WHAT THE **IDES:**

A very worthy vsradio

Easily carried ... *...ravel library. The authors wax as enthusiastically as I do about the almost too-quaint-to-believe Country Inns.* **—San Francisco Chronicle**

Armed with these guides, you may never again stay in a conventional hotel. **—Travelore Report**

Charming, extremely informative, clear and easy to read; excellent travelling companions. **—Books-Across-The-Sea** *(The English Speaking Union)*

This series of pocket-sized paperbacks will guide travelers to hundreds of little known and out of the way inns, lodges, and historic hotels. . . . a thorough menu. **—(House Beautiful's) Colonial Homes**

The beautiful English countryside is made even prettier. . . . This book lists English inns stayed in by such famous guests as Charles Dickens, William Wordsworth, Oscar Wilde and countless others. . . . **—Dallas (TX.) Morning News**

We commend the book to you if you're planning a trip to Great Britain any time soon. . . . It's complete and makes easy reading, even for the armchair traveler. **—United Retirement Bulletin**

If you . . . turn all funny at the sight of ancient beams and polished brass, [this] new book will guide you to the best in Britain. **—Chattanooga (Tenn.) News-Free Press**

It is very seldom a travel book comes along reading like a letter from a highly literate friend . . . [This] treasure of a travel book. . . . was written with love and discrimination by a pair of inveterate travelers who enjoy charm and history but who also appreciate the creature comforts we all look for. **—Greenwich (Conn.) Time**

Brings a great deal more to the subject [than other guides]. . . . Names of the inns alone are worth a thumbing trip through the book.

One can only welcome such guide books and wish them long, happy, and healthy lives in print. **—Wichita (Kansas) Eagle**

The [authors], sharing a dislike of chain hotels, sought out older, sometimes historic inns that combine architectural character with good service and comfortable surroundings. **—Providence (R.I.) Journal**

Very fine travel guides. **—Santa Ana (Calif.) Register**

A wonderful source for planning trips. **—Northampton (Mass.) Gazette**

. . . pocketsize books full of facts. . . . attractively made and illustrated. **—New York Times Book Review**

ALSO AVAILABLE IN THE COMPLEAT TRAVELER SERIES

Great Britain

COUNTRY INNS
Castles & Historic Hotels

Eileen & Eugene O'Reilly

BURT FRANKLIN & COMPANY, INC.

Published by
BURT FRANKLIN & COMPANY
P.O. Box 856
New York, New York 10014

NINETH EDITION

Library of Congress Cataloging in Publication Data

O'Reilly, Eileen
Country Inns and historic hotels of Great Britain.

(The compleat traveler's companion)
Includes index.
1. Hotels, taverns, etc.—Great Britain—Direct
ories. I. O'Reilly, Eugene.
II. Title. III. Series: Compleat traveler's
companion.
TX910.G7037   1989   647'.944101
ISBN 0-89102-400-x (pbk.)

Cover Photo: Ye Olde Bell at Hurley
Printed in the United States of America

1 3 5 4 2

CONTENTS

WALES

CONTENTS

INTRODUCTION

TO THOSE WHO DELIGHT in independent travel we offer this book and wish them happy journeys, sunny adventures, meetings with interesting strangers, and a warm welcome at the end of the day.

Enjoying a lodging is a highly subjective pleasure. We cannot tell you where to go; we can only tell you where we have been and why we liked it, hoping that you can choose from our descriptions those places that are right for you. Accommodations range from some of the most luxurious hotels in Britain to homespun, relatively inexpensive little inns, each with its own kind of appeal. When we travel we enjoy experiencing another time as well as another place, so all of these hotels are legacies of an earlier age, some of them incredibly old, others from the more recent past.

It was only after some hesitation that we decided to criticize a little here and there certain minor drawbacks, since it seemed not quite "nice" to find fault with some aspect of a pleasant place where the innkeeper was working hard to please. We ourselves, along with other members of our family, are owners of an inn, the Inn at Castle Hill in Newport, Rhode Island. We do not manage it—it is leased—but we are well aware of the hard work that is required to run an inn successfully. We were told by the author of a guide to American inns never to criticize—just recommend or leave out. But very few, if any, hotels are perfect. We have been disappointed with a lodging, glowingly described in some guidebook, that we might have enjoyed had there not been such a discrepancy between expectation and fact. An overrated place is a letdown, whereas the same place can be enjoyed (or avoided) when the drawbacks are expected.

In some good hotels you will find atmospheric public rooms but bedrooms that are not well decorated. We use the work "plain" to describe rooms that are clean and comfortable but decorated without style or charm. We have been pleased with every one of these lodgings, slept in some and eaten in others, and discussed them with other travelers recently returned from visits to them.

We do not name the more than five hundred hotels, usually well recommended, that we checked and found wanting. Some were so badly modernized, architecturally or decoratively, that we could only shudder and keep repeating, "What a pity!" Orange plastic and rock music in a historic inn are somehow not unlike a grandmother in a bikini. Other inns, though atmospheric, were musty. Even the most dedicated antiquarian finds little romantic about antique smells. Many of the inns were adequate but without charm, and at one otherwise lovely Cotswold manor the staff seemed to find the guests an unfortunate nuisance.

Although care has been taken to make sure our information is correct, there will inevitably be some changes after this book has gone to press—a hotel closed or sold, opening later or closing earlier in the season, an increase in price. *We strongly recommend that you use the most current edition of this guide when traveling since there are constant changes from year to year.* Price categories listed in the text should be considered only as indications of the relative cost of the establishments. Rates should always be checked when making reservations.

We like to receive reports from our readers on their experiences with these hotels. Your reader reports are the best way for us to keep track of the performance of each lodging. You can write to us at Box 484R, Newport, Rhode Island, 02840. We would also welcome hearing about our readers' own favorites.

TRAVEL TIPS

OUR EXPERIENCE INDICATES THAT it is best to have a reservation for the first night no matter how much of a vagabond you fancy yourself; to spend that night no more than 40 miles from the airport, preferably nearer, if you are renting a car there; and to reserve rooms ahead if you plan to stop over in a city. Driving and parking are too difficult to allow a search for a hotel room. If you arrive early in the day and don't like what you find, you can search further before registering. It may be worth it to you to change lodgings and lose a deposit. On the other hand, you may be more satisfied with what you have reserved once you have seen the alternatives.

The idea of driving through the countryside and stopping at some cozy little inn when the mood strikes has a fine romantic lilt to it, and that was the way we wanted to travel. We gradually learned that it was far more romantic to sleep in a four-poster in a famous smugglers' inn, where we had reserved in advance, than it was to spend the night in a commercial hotel because everything romantic was already taken.

We prefer to travel to Great Britain on British Airways. When we hear the distinctive British voices of the flight attendants, we feel that our British experience has already begun. We have found that we can reserve our car at a discount if we make arrangements through the airline at the time we book our flight; if we want, we can return that car at the airport in either Glasgow, Edinburgh, or Manchester without a drop-off penalty and take a British Airways shuttle that connects with our flight home from London.

To ensure an answer when you write abroad for a reservation, include an international reply coupon that you have purchased from your post office. Many hotels, especially small guest houses, cannot afford to pay postage to tell you, and perhaps dozens of others, that they are already full on the dates you require. We find that if we include a deposit in the form of a personal check, we are more likely to secure a reservation. If the lodging cannot take you, it will return the deposit. We make a few reservations ahead before we leave home if we especially want to stay in some hotels we know to be so highly recommended they are always booked well in advance. We leave nights open between reservations for flexibility and for the unexpected find that might be marvelous. We have learned to start looking for a lodging by 3 P.M. Sometimes we find a room in an inn we like on our first try. Sometimes we do not. Then we have time to drive on and seek another. The most unsatisfactory lodgings we've stayed in were the ones we checked in to after 5 P.M. By then the charmers are often full. After hearing three or four times that there is no room at the inn, the tendency is to settle for the first clean place that will take you. In season it is wise to have your hotel telephone ahead for a reservation in some recommended place. A popular hotel is more likely to accept an unsecured reservation from another hotel than from you, a stranger. Hotels expect to telephone for you. Don't wait until you are checking out to ask them to, however, as it can take a while for calls to go through. And be sure to telephone and cancel as early as possible if something keeps you from reaching that reserved room.

It has been said that no European takes a room without first inspecting it, while Americans ask for a room with a bath and take whatever they are assigned. If the hotel is full, you will obviously have no selection, but we suggest that you always ask upon arrival to see other rooms. We have often preferred a master bedroom in an old manor house, with the bath down the hall, to a more modern and more expensive small room with a private bath recently converted from servants' quarters. Two rooms sharing one bath may be more desirable than the two with private baths—excellent if you are traveling with another couple. You may also decide you don't like any of the rooms, and if you reach this decision by 3 P.M., the hotel will have time to rent the room again, and you can feel free to drive on to find lodging elsewhere.

One of the easiest ways to save money is to take a room without a private bath. As an innkeeper once said to me, "Most Americans think that taking a room without a private bath is positively *un-American*." Perhaps they have visions of standing in a hallway dressed in a bathrobe, toothbrush in hand, waiting in line to get into the bathroom. We have never seen, much less experienced, such a scene. There is usually a washbasin in a bedroom without a private bathroom, and there is almost always more than one hall bathroom. In Britain, unlike some countries in Continental Europe, hall bathrooms are not kept locked, and you do not have to make an appointment or pay to take a bath. Some of the most luxurious hotels in this guide have some rooms without private bath, and the difference in price can be up to 36 pounds a night.

We suggest you plan to stay about 100 miles from your previous lodging. You will be on back roads that twist and turn—or if you aren't, you should be. Your actual mileage will be more, because you will detour to see historic and scenic spots along the way. You will take time to go into a museum, a garden, an ancient little church, a magnificent cathedral. If you feel like more driving after you have settled into an inn, there is nothing to prevent you from exploring the surrounding countryside.

We are told, "But I must see as much as possible. I may not get there again." What you will see will be more highways. Distances covered are not important, but quality of experience is. We find that a stay of about three days in each lodging is the most enjoyable way to go. It is delightful to return after a day of sightseeing to join other guests you have already met—to have the staff greet you by name and ask after your day's meandering. Also, many hotels give a reduced rate for a stay of two, three, or more days, usually on the modified American plan (MAP), which includes dinner. Always establish what plan you are taking before you register. If you decide after a day to move on, you can simply pay the one-day rate and leave. But if you register for the bed and breakfast rate and then decide to stay on, you cannot always get the reduced rate.

You will absorb the atmosphere of Britain far more by spending an occasional day out of your car, browsing in an antique store, having tea and scones in a little shop where the other seats are occupied by local housewives laden with string shopping bags, or eating lunch in the local pub, where it is easy to converse with the natives if you ask a few questions about the town's sights or history. Remember that in British pubs patrons are not seated separately. You find a seat at any table that has room. You walk to the bar to get your own drinks and pay for these as you receive them, not when you are through eating. Neither teetotalers nor unescorted ladies should hesitate to eat in pubs. We talked with an Australian couple at our hotel one evening who said their only problem was finding a place to get a light lunch. When we asked if they hadn't lunched in pubs, they said they didn't drink. We assured them that soft drinks are dispensed almost as frequently as alcoholic beverages at lunchtime in pubs.

Despite our love for back roads, we have to say that it is sometimes best to get on the superhighways. On our first trip we were determined not to use them. We would see the "real" Britain. Many trips later, we know that when we want to get around a city or go through an industrial area the superhighway is the only way to go. The alternative roads are the "real" Britain, all right. They are just as real as any road leading into an American city, clogged with traffic and lined with shopping malls, used-car lots, building complexes, and restaurants and nightclubs with neon signs. They are the kind of commercial enterprises necessary to any city but not what we go to Britain to see.

SOME THINGS TO
TAKE WITH YOU

Sectional road maps of Great Britain. We cannot emphasize too strongly how necessary we feel these to be. Every back road is drawn in, as are most small villages. These maps are hard to find in the United States, although two sources are Forsyth Travel Library, 9154 West 57th Street, Shawnee Mission, Kansas, 55201; telephone: (800) 367-7984 and Book Passage, 51 Tamal Vista Boulevard, Corte Madera, California, 94925; telephone: (800) 321-9785. If you do not bring them with you, buy them as soon as you arrive. We like the Shell maps, divided into seven areas besides London. Most gas stations sell them, as well as some bookstores.

A single map of all Great Britain. The British Tourist Authority at 40 West 57th Street, New York, New York 10019, will send one free that has scenic areas marked. It will also send a London map.

We like to carry an atlas to Britain also. The index is helpful in finding small villages that may be hard to locate on even the area maps. You can buy one in Britain, ask your local bookstore to order one, or write to The British Travel Bookshop, 40 West 57th Street, New York, New York 10019, phone (212) 765-0898. It might seem that with an atlas you won't need the individual maps. On the maps, however, it is easier to see several counties at once. With the atlas you must keep flipping pages, and there may be times when you want an overall picture of a larger area.

An *electrical converter set*, a small folding high-intensity *lamp*, and an *extension cord*. If you like to read in bed, don't count on a good reading light in every country inn. Sometimes all you will need is a 100-watt bulb to replace the 25-watt bulb you may find in the inn's bedside lamp. You must buy one when you get to Britain, as American bulbs do not fit British lamp sockets.

Other items we have found useful include a plastic bottle of detergent (you can buy one after you arrive), a travel clothesline with suction cups, inflatable plastic clothes hangers, a plastic cleaner's bag to place under dripping laundry (packed between folds of clothing in your suitcase it helps keep wrinkles away), a roll of large plastic bags (for enclosing damp laundry and many other uses), a sewing kit and a Buttoneer (for attaching buttons without sewing), a travel alarm clock, a small flashlight, eyeglass prescriptions.

HOW TO READ THE LISTINGS

Breaks	Special rates apply for a two- or three-day stay at certain times. The package includes meals and sometimes a tour, activity, or free use of some special facility.
Children free sharing	Children sharing a room with two adults are not charged except for meals taken.
Cocktail bar Public bar	While some cocktail bars are for the use of the resident guests only, others also serve the public. In general, the atmosphere of a cocktail bar is more luxurious than that of a public bar. A public bar is heavily patronized by local people.
Credit cards	In Great Britain MasterCard is called Access and Visa is called Barclaycard.
Double room	When asking for a double room, specify whether you will accept a double bed, twin beds, or either. (We have been told, "No, we have no double room, only one with twin beds.")
Early and late snacks	Snacks are usually served just at lunchtime. Where we say, "early and late," they are served at suppertime also or, rarely, all afternoon and into the evening.
Fishing and shooting	Fishing and shooting are listed only under hotels that advise that gear can be rented or borrowed.
Golf	Golf is listed only under hotels that state that golf clubs can be rented or borrowed. If you have your own clubs, there is hardly a lodging that can't arrange for you to play golf on one of the more than 1,800 golf courses in Britain.
Ground-floor rooms Elevator	Though not necessarily suitable for guests dependent on wheelchairs, accommodations so labeled are desirable for those who do not want to climb stairs. Never

ask for a room on the first floor if you want to be on the ground floor. In Britain, the first floor is the floor above the ground floor — what Americans call the second floor.

How to get there	If no detailed directions are given, the hotel will be easy to find in the center of the village. We do not give directions in London. (When driving into London, we have hired a taxi on the outskirts to lead us to our rental-car drop-off place. The taxi then takes us to our hotel.)

When the hotel will meet guests at an airport or railway station, there will be a charge unless otherwise noted, and arrangements must be made with the hotel when reserving your room. |
Hunting	The hotel will arrange for the guest to join a hunt.
Luncheon	Luncheon is a sit-down meal served in a dining room.
Off-season rates	Off-season rates vary among hotels, with some raising rates at Easter, others as late as July. Rates could be reduced anytime from September to January.
Rates	Prices can go out of date soon after a guide is published. We note under the description of each lodging a comparative price rating so the reader can know how it compares in price to all others in the guide. Some hotels will fall into two categories because some of their rooms are more expensive than others. These prices are for two people in the 1988 high season and include breakfast (usually a full breakfast but in a few cases a Continental breakfast), service, and tax. *Actual rates are listed in the index.*

very inexpensive	up to £30
inexpensive	£31 to £43
moderate	£44 to £70
expensive	£71 to £100
very expensive	more than £100

Reduction	A reduction is made for a stay of two or three days all year, usually MAP (Modified American Plan), which includes dinner. Always establish the rate and plan before registering.

Restaurant service	All meals listed under each entry are served to the general public, not just to house guests. All lodgings recommended in this book serve breakfast to house guests. All serve dinner to house guests unless noted otherwise in the write-up of that lodging. In addition, many serve luncheon, snacks, or tea to house guests but not to the general public. All lodgings in this guide serve licensed beverages to both restaurant and house guests unless noted otherwise in the write-up.

The listings do not necessarily apply on Sunday. Some hotels serve only a large traditional dinner Sunday at midday. They may not be open on Sunday evening, or they may serve a cold buffet, sometimes only to house guests. Few serve snacks or tea on Sunday.

Snacks	A snack is a light meal, sometimes just bread and cheese (called a ploughman's lunch), sometimes sandwiches, hot soup, meat pies, and occasionally a buffet from which you choose and pay for only what you want. It is usually served in a tavern or pub but sometimes on a tray in a lounge and often, in good weather, outside. (Our first day in England we began to feel rejected when three pubs told us they could not give us lunch, and at the third one there were sandwiches made up at the bar. "Can't we buy some of those?" we asked. "Oh, *snacks*! Of course, dear, you can have *snacks*. We don't have *lunch*. But I could cook you some nice ham and eggs if you'd like." Unless you want a formal meal served in a dining room, don't ask for lunch.)
Supper	Supper is a light dinner, called high tea in Britain, usually served before the dinner hour or, in a few hotels, in a second dining room that serves only light meals.
[T]	The hotel will pay a travel agent a commission on rooms. The percentage varies among hotels.
Tea	Afternoon tea includes such items as scones, tea sandwiches, or cake — not just a commercially baked cookie (which is called a biscuit).
Tea-making	The bedroom is equipped with facilities to make tea and coffee (electric kettle, cups, spoons, tea bags, instant coffee, sugar and creamer).

Telephone	The number in parentheses is the STD, or area, code. Most places in Great Britain can be dialed direct from America. For instructions ask the operator.
U.S. Agents	Some British hotels are represented by the following American agents. You or your travel agent may call these for reservations for the hotels that list an American agent. Sometimes only the hotel's more expensive rooms are handled by the agent.

Abercrombie and Kent International, Inc. (800) 323-7308; in Illinois, collect, (312) 954-2944; Fax, (312) 954-3324.
Best Western (800) 528-1234.
BTH (800) 221-1074; Canada, (800) 344-4034.
David Mitchell & Company, Inc., (800) 372-1323; in New York State, (212) 696-1323; Fax, (212) 213-2297.
Josephine Barr (800) 323-5463; in Illinois, (312) 251-4110.
Ray Morrow Associates (800) 243-9420; in Virginia, (804) 460-2343
Romantik (Hotels) (800) 826-0015; in Seattle, (206)486-9394
Scott Calder (800) 223-6764; in New York State, (212) 535-9530 collect; in Canada, (800) 346-8480.
Selective Hotels (800) 223-6764; in New York State, (800) 522-5568; in New York City, (212) 714-2323.
THF (Trust Houses Forte) (800) 223-5672; Fax, (913) 831-1523.

With bath	Specify if a private bathroom with tub *or* shower is acceptable. (We have been told, "No, we have no room with a private bath, only one with a shower.") Occasionally, a private bathroom must be reached through a public hall. If it is important for you to have a private bathroom opening directly into your bedroom, specify a bathroom *en suite*.

NORTHERN ENGLAND AND SCOTLAND

SECTION 3

SCOTLAND

NORTH SEA

NORTH CHANNEL

Glasgow Edinburgh

Newcastle

IRISH SEA

SECTION 4

York

Leeds

Liverpool

Manchester

Sheffield

Nottingham

The Wash

Cardigan Bay

W A L E S

E N G L A N D

Saint George's Channel

Birmingham

Norwich

Ipswich

Bristol Channel

Bristol

London

STRAIT OF DOVER

Southampton

Brighton

Plymouth

Isle of Wight

SECTION 1

ENGLISH CHANNEL

SECTION 2

SOUTHERN ENGLAND AND WALES

MAP BY IRA KENNEDY

SECTION 1

NORTH SEA

● Lincoln

● Rowsley

Weybourne ●

● Grimsthorpe

E   N   G

Stamford ●

L

A

Bishops Tachbrook

● Wilmcote

● Bury St Edmunds

N

● Stratford-upon-Avon

Chipping Campden

Lavenham ●

● Aldeburgh

Blockley

Long Melford ●

D

● Moreton-in-March

● Dedham

● Upper Slaughter

Aston Clinton

● Horton-cum-Studley ●

● Burford

Bibury

● Dorchester-on-Thames

Henley-on-Thames ●   ● Hurley

London

★

R. Thames

Canterbury ●

Goudhurst ●   ● Cranbrook

● East Grinstead

● Hawkhurst

Rye ●

...dhurst

Midhurst ●

● Arundel

●

● Bosham

S

Isle of

Wight

Climping

Bonchurch

CHANNEL

L   I   S   H

SOUTHERN ENGLAND AND WALES

SECTION 2

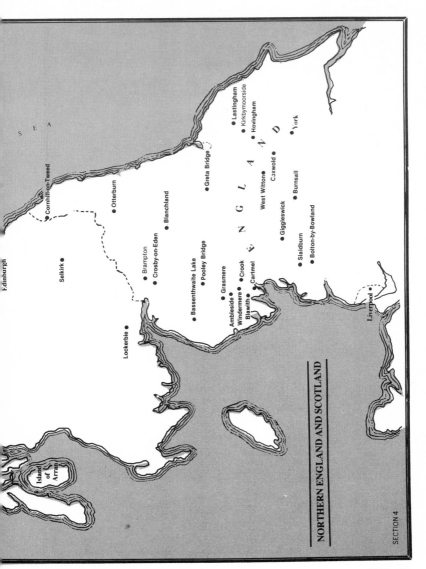

SECTION 4

NORTHERN ENGLAND AND SCOTLAND

Edinburgh

Island
of
Arran

Lockerbie ●

Selkirk ●

S E A

Cornhill-on-Tweed ●

● Otterburn

● Brampton
● Crosby-on-Eden

● Blanchland

● Greta Bridge

● Lastingham
● Kirkbymoorside
● Hovingham

● York

E N G L A N D

● Bassenthwaite Lake
● Pooley Bridge

West Witton ● Coxwold ●

● Grasmere

● Giggleswick ● Burnsall

● Ambleside
● Windermere ● Crook
● Blawith ● Cartmel

● Slaidburn
● Bolton-by-Bowland

Liverpool ●

ENGLAND

LIST OF TOWNS BY REGION

Readers interested in visiting a particular region will find it listed below with the names of its towns in alphabetical order as they appear in the text.

The Cotswolds and Shakespeare Country: Bibury, Bishops Tachbrook, Blockley, Broadway, Burford, Cheltenham, Chipping Campden, Moreton-in-Marsh, Shurdington, Stratford-upon-Avon, Tetbury, Upper Slaughter, Westonbirt, Wilmcote

East Anglia: Aldeburgh, Bury St. Edmunds, Dedham, Lavenham, Long Melford, Weybourne

The East Midlands: Grimsthorpe, Lincoln, Rowsley, Stamford

The Lake District: Ambleside, Bassenthwaite Lake, Blawith, Brampton, Cartmel, Crook, Crosby-on-Eden, Grasmere, Pooley Bridge, Windermere

Lancashire: Bolton-by-Bowland, Slaidburn

The Marches: Abberley, Diddlebury, Ledbury, Ludlow, Ullingswick, Welland

Northumbria: Blanchland, Cornhill-on-Tweed, Otterburn

South East England: Canterbury, Cranbrook, East Grinstead, Goudhurst, Hawkhurst, Rye

Southern England: Arundel, Bonchurch, Bosham, Climping, Lyndhurst, Midhurst, Salisbury

Thames and Chilterns: Aston Clinton, Dorchester-on-Thames, Henley-on-Thames, Horton-cum-Studley, Hurley, London

The West Country: Beanacre, Bovey Tracey, Branscombe, Chagford, Constantine Bay, Crackington Haven, Evershot, Frampton, Gittisham, Helford, Huntsham, Kilve, Lacock, Lifton, Poughill, St. Austell, South Zeal, Sturminster Newton, Thornbury, Wells

Yorkshire: Burnsall, Coxwold, Giggleswick, Greta Bridge, Hovingham, Kildwick, Kirkbymoorside, Lastingham, West Witton, York

Abberley, Hereford and Worcester

ELMS

A thing of beauty is a joy forever.

John Keats

This beautiful building, constructed in 1710 in the reign of Queen Anne and designed by a pupil of the renowned Sir Christopher Wren, is a building of special architectural interest. It looks very grand and formal, but a warm country welcome awaits the traveler.

When we arrived at teatime, a wood fire burned gently. The high-ceilinged drawing room held books and fresh flowers. One could imagine that Edith Wharton and Henry James were among the guests sitting on the velvet chairs and tufted sofas.

A wide, thickly carpeted oak staircase leads to bedrooms with spectacular views. The Library Bar, which retains its fine old mahogany bookcases, in warm weather opens onto the adjacent terrace overlooking the 12 acres of parkland, formal gardens, and putting green. All the rooms contain handsome paintings and interesting oddments, such as a mahogany knife box converted to a depository for outgoing mail. Candlelight dinners in the Regency dining room have been recommended in British food guides.

Yesterday lingers gracefully at the Elms, a good choice for those for whom travel means staying in places they aren't likely to forget.

Proprietor: Ms. Mooney. *Recreational facilities:* Tennis and putting green at the hotel. *Other facilities:* 2 drawing rooms, lounge, cocktail bar, garden, laundry service. *Rooms:* 25 with bath, TV, and telephone; suites. Suitable for wheelchair guests. Weekend breaks; Christmas program. No children under 3. Expensive. *Restaurant service:* Luncheon, dinner (coat and tie). *Credit cards:* All. *How to get there:* Abberley is about 10 miles northwest of Worcester. Leave Route M5 at exit 7. The Elms is on Route A443. *Telephone:* (0299) 896666. *Agent in the United States:* Scott Calder. [T]

UPLANDS HOTEL

> I belong at home in Aldeburgh . . . all the music I
> write comes from it.
>
> *Benjamin Britten*

This unpretentious, pleasant hotel was the childhood home of Elizabeth Garrett Anderson, Britain's first woman doctor. The living rooms are like those of a private house, with magazines and books about. At the informal bar, one evening, some jolly Englishmen, down for golf, each wanted to buy the Americans an after-dinner drink.

Delicious food, which attracts many area patrons, is served in a dining room that is larger and more formal than the rest of the hotel. We much prefer the bedrooms in the main house to the small, motel-like rooms built in the garden.

Several operas by Benjamin Britten, eminent composer and Aldeburgh native, were performed for the first time at the famous Aldeburgh Festival, held each June. Boats to sail, row, canoe, or punt can be hired at a lake safe for children, as can sailboats on the River Alde, with instruction if desired.

Shops line the streets paralleling the sea at this small seaside resort, where fishing boats go out from the beach. We did not care for any of the beachfront hotels but were very happy at Uplands.

Proprietors: Robert, Patricia, and Nichola Tidder. *Recreational facilities:* Swimming and tennis a short walk away; golf a short drive away. *Other facilities:* Lounge, TV lounge, sun parlor, cocktail bar, garden. *Rooms:* 20 with bath, telephone, TV, and tea-making. Ground-floor rooms. Winter breaks; Christmas program. Moderate. *Restaurant service:* Luncheon, dinner. *Credit cards:* Amex, Master, Visa. *How to get there:* Aldeburgh is on the Suffolk coast. The hotel is on Victoria Road (Route 1094) at the edge of town. *Telephone:* (072 885) 2420.

Ambleside, Cumbria

NAB COTTAGE

> We passed The Nab, in which De Quincey formerly
> lived, and where Hartley Coleridge lived and died. It
> is a small, buff-tinted, plastered stone cottage, I should
> think of a very humble class originally; but it now
> looks as if persons of taste might sometime or other
> have set down in it, and caused flowers to spring up
> about it.
>
> *Nathaniel Hawthorne,* 1854

Nab Cottage, crowded with literary associations, brings memories of
the poets who made the Lake District so famous. It was the farm home
of the girl Thomas De Quincey married after their child was born. The
marriage was a happy one, although De Quincey was dropped by his
friends the Wordsworths, partly for marrying a "low-class woman."
Some years afterward he lived in the house with his family. When they
moved away, Wordsworth arranged a lease on it for Hartley Coleridge,

beloved schoolmaster in the village, the talented but ill-fated son of Samuel Taylor Coleridge and nephew of Robert Southey. Then the Wordsworth family visited Nab Cottage frequently.

The house is across the road from Rydal Lake, where Wordsworth liked to ice-skate. A desk reputed to have belonged to Coleridge is among the furnishings at Nab Cottage, and all its bedrooms hold some old pieces. A home-cooked dinner is offered. Among the guests who gather for evening tea before a coal fire in the lounge are many who return year after year, some revisiting the house where they stayed as children. Professors of literature are particularly drawn to the inn.

If you take the short walk to Rydal Mount, Wordsworth's last home and now a museum, you can almost see the poet striding along the road, his faithful sister Dorothy by his side, sometimes speaking aloud as he tries out a line of verse evolving in his head. At Rydal Mount you can picture him seated there surrounded by the women who waited on him so devotedly: sister, wife, daughter, sister-in-law. The peace and simplicity of the England of the poets cling to Nab Cottage and its surroundings.

Proprietor: Jean Melling. *Closed:* December through February. *Recreational facilities:* Indoor pool, lake swimming, tennis, squash, riding, boat rental, and boat trips a short drive away. *Facilities for children:* Baby-sitting and -listening. *Other facilities:* Lounge, TV lounge, garden. *Rooms:* 7 sharing baths. Winter breaks. Reduction for children sharing (under 2 free). Very inexpensive. *How to get there:* Nab Cottage is on Route A591 between Grasmere and Ambleside. *Telephone:* (096 65) 311.

ROTHAY MANOR

Our road lay through Ambleside, which is certainly a very pretty town, and looks cheerfully in a sunny day.

Nathaniel Hawthorne, 1854

This refined Regency house, relaxed and friendly with its flower-laden atmosphere, is filled with paintings and prints, antiques that range from carved Jacobean mirrors to Victorian chairs, and those tipsy, elaborate lampshades that we love in Europe and that would look hilarious if we took them back home. Log fires are lighted on chilly days. Outside the sunny bay windows, white garden furniture looks irresistible beside flower beds and a croquet lawn under imposing old trees.

A winter program provides special dinners on Wednesdays and Fridays. Cooking and wines from various regions of France are featured, along with wine tastings and demonstrations of such crafts as furniture restoration using antique tools and glass engraving. In mid-December there is an evening of nostalgia when guests are welcomed with steaming drinks before listening to "Charles Dickens" read passages from his latest works. Then all sit to a dinner of roast Michaelmas goose and plum pudding, after which the young at heart play Victorian games like blind man's bluff and forfeits. For those who don't like to move around every day, this well-run hotel would be a delightful base from which to explore England's Lake District.

Proprietors: Nigel and Stephen Nixon. *Closed:* Early January to mid-February. *Recreational facilities:* Lake and river swimming and tennis a short walk away; coarse and trout fishing, riding, hunting, squash, and lake steamer a short drive away. *Facilities for children:* Children's supper. *Other facilities:* Drawing room, lounge, cocktail bar, garden. *Rooms:* 18 with bath, TV, telephone; 3 suites. Suitable for wheelchair guests. Off-season rates; breaks; 4-day Christmas program; 3-day New Year's program. Minimum two nights on weekends. Expensive. *Restaurant service:* Luncheon, tea, dinner. *Credit cards:* Amex, Diners, Master, Visa. *How to get there:* From Ambleside, at the northern tip of Lake Windermere, find Rothay Manor on the road marked "to Coniston." *Telephone:* (0966) 33605. *Agent in the United States:* Josephine Barr.

Arundel, West Sussex
NORFOLK ARMS

> As they reach the foot of the hill, the guard commences a solo on his bugle, to give notice to the innkeeper to have the coach dinner on the table.
>
> *Robert Surtees,* 1831

Great was the glamour of the coaching age. On the steep High Street rising from the River Arun, the Norfolk Arms once knew the music of the guard's horn as the coach swept under the archway into the stable yard.

The centuries have been kind to the Norfolk Arms. Some of the bedrooms contain four-posters, and the main hall is enhanced by many antiques. While less personal that a small, owner-operated hotel, it has a friendly staff.

Arundel is one of the loveliest towns in southern England. Its ancient buildings cluster beneath the towers of majestic, historic Arundel Castle, ancestral home of the dukes of Norfolk. No family in English history has a more tumultuous past than the enormously wealthy Norfolks, whose lives have been entwined with those of royalty through centuries of ancient plots and intrigues. The castle has withstood siege three times. Beside it is a Roman Catholic cathedral, for the Norfolks were one of the few titled families that held to the old religion. You may go through the castle and its park, and you'll enjoy the antique shops along the High Street.

Manager: David Horridge. *Recreational facilities:* Ocean swimming, tennis, riding, golf, and boat rental a short drive away. *Facilities for children:* Children's supper. *Other facilities:* Lounge, cocktail bar. *Rooms:* 34 with bath, TV, video movies, telephone, and tea-making. Suitable for wheelchair guests. 2-day reduction; free for children under 15 sharing. Moderate. *Restaurant service:* Luncheon, early and late snacks, dinner. *Credit cards:* Amex, Diners, Master, Visa. *How to get there:* Guests can be met at the Arundel railway station. *Telephone:* (0903) 882101. [T]

Aston Clinton, Buckinghamshire

BELL INN

> Alas! Alas! Where is it gone,
> That coach with its four bright bays?
> Alas! Alas! Where is it gone
> That spicey team of greys?
>
> *C. Birch Reynardson,* 1875

There are no coaches and horses outside the Bell today; you are much more likely to see a helicopter hovering among the trees, ready to land a guest. An officially listed historic building, once part of the estate of the Duke of Buckingham and known as an inn since at least 1650, the Bell has been developed into one of the most prestigious hostelries in Britain.

In 1939, it was bought by Gerard Harris, a lawyer by profession but a gourmet and restaurateur by inclination, a man "passionately interested in food and wine." It is now run by the Harris family and improving all the time, if that is possible. While there are always traditional British dishes—poached Scotch salmon, tipsy cake—and game in season, such as pheasant, wild duck, hare, venison, and partridge, fine French cooking predominates. It was a favorite of Evelyn Waugh's. The dining room draws discerning Londoners, so make a dinner reservation when you reserve your room.

Antique furnishings have been chosen as for a private house. Fourteen of the rooms are in converted stables and malt houses around a cobbled courtyard. Some have doors opening onto a garden, and each has fresh-flower arrangements, bath salts, a bathroom scale, those luxurious terry robes sometimes found in expensive European hotels, and a refrigerator stocked with drinks.

The inn is on a busy road in a fairly built-up area close to London, not far from Heathrow, and would be a grand place for a bang-up splurge your last night.

Proprietor: Michael Harris. *Rooms:* 21 with bath, TV, and telephone. Suitable for wheelchair guests. Discounts for children under 16 sharing. Expensive. *Restaurant service:* Luncheon, snacks, dinner. *Credit cards:* Master, Visa. *How to get there:* The inn is on Route A41, 4 miles east of Aylesbury. *Telephone:* (0296) 630252. *Agent in the United States:* David Mitchell.　　　　　　　　　　　　　　　[T]

PHEASANT INN

> D'ye ken John Peel with his coat so gay?
> D'ye ken John Peel at the break of day?
> D'ye ken John Peel when he's far far away
> With his hounds and his horn in the morning?
>
> *John Graves,* 1828

For pure charm, the Pheasant is a winner. The time-blackened beams and white plaster walls of this sixteenth-century inn give great character to rooms filled with groupings of chintz-covered chairs. Everything is bright and cheerful. Walls are decked with guns, sporting prints, blue and white china, and oil paintings. Welcoming fires and a "taste of England" menu are other attractions.

Local people like the original bar, where real ale is on tap. Electric blankets and full central heating keep visitors warm and comfortable all winter. To top it all, the price is right. The Pheasant Inn was a hangout for the legendary John Peel. The type of fox hunting for which he was famous—on foot, not horseback—starts in front of the inn. If you can't stay, stop in for afternoon tea, in the garden in good weather.

Manager: William Barrington-Wilson. *Closed:* Christmas. *Recreational facilities:* Lake swimming, free golf, riding, hunting, boat rental, and boat trips nearby. *Other facilities:* 3 lounges, public bar, garden. *Rooms:* 20 with bath. 3-bedroom self-catering cottage. Suitable for wheelchair guests. 3-day reduction; 2-day breaks; reduction for children sharing. Moderate. *Restaurant service:* Luncheon, snacks, tea, dinner (no smoking). *How to get there:* The inn is just off Route A66 at the head of Bassenthwaite Lake between Keswick and Cockermouth. *Telephone:* (059 681) 234.

BEECHFIELD HOUSE

> Quality is never an accident. It is always the result of
> intelligent effort.
>
> *John Ruskin,* 1870

We followed a tree-lined drive bordered with daffodils to a stone mansion called Beechfield House and entered a world of Victorian elegance. The gracious atmosphere here is friendly and relaxed. Richard Burton and Cary Grant are counted among past guests.

Crystal chandeliers sparkle, and log fires cast a glow over rooms furnished with Georgian and Victorian antiques. Large bedrooms decorated in soft colors, some with four-poster beds, have comfortable sitting areas. Peter's experience as an international chef is responsible for the quality of the busy restaurant, recommended in all food guides. You'll have a choice of classical French or regional English dishes, along with an outstanding list of over 300 wines. House guests may order a light snack at any time from 8 A.M. to 10 P.M.

Two acres of garden and orchard supply the kitchen. A heated swimming pool in a walled garden is open from April through September, and a grass tennis court and a croquet lawn invite play. The River Avon almost borders the eight acres, and a pleasure not to miss is the two-mile walk along Avon's public towpath to the village of Lacock.

Manager: Robert Smith. *Recreational facilities:* Tennis and outdoor pool at the house; boat trips on the River Avon, river and lake fishing, riding, hunting, squash, and sauna nearby. *Facilities for children:* Baby-sitting and -listening; children's supper. *Other facilities:* Drawing room, sitting room, garden. *Rooms:* 16 with bath, telephone and TV; suitable for wheel-chair guests; minimum 2-night stay on weekends. Winter breaks November through March; Christmas program. Expensive. *Restaurant service:* Luncheon, tea, dinner. *Credit cards:* Amex, Diners, Master, Visa. *How to get there:* The house is on Route A350 between Melksham and Lacock. *Telephone:* (0225) 703700.   [T]

BIBURY COURT

> We procured the key of the church—a key the size
> of Dover Castle—and admired it as lightsome, and
> well-glazed.
>
> *John Byng,* 1794

A door in the wall of Bibury Court's garden leads into the churchyard
of a Saxon church admired by John Byng during his visit long ago to
beautiful Bibury. This great house was built in 1633 by Sir Thomas
Sackville, illegitimate son of the first earl of Dorset and a "Knight and
gentleman-usher in dailie waiting on the King." Its spacious rooms are
furnished in the styles of different periods, from bedrooms with Jacobean oak four-posters to the cocktail lounge decorated in the 1920s in
Art Nouveau style. A spirit of jollity prevails in a bar in the coach house
where local people congregate. Tea is served in the garden in summer.

If the ghost of Charles II, said to have been a visitor at Bibury Court,
wanders through the corridors, is he astonished at today's world, where
anyone with the price of a night's lodging can slumber in chambers once
reserved for nobles? Would the easygoing, affable Charles approve?
You will. You can't help but feel welcome here.

Proprietor: James Collier. *Closed:* Christmas. *Special facilities:*
Lounge, TV lounge, cocktail bar, public bar, garden. *Rooms:* 15 with
bath and telephone. Winter breaks. Moderate. *Restaurant service:*
Snacks, dinner. *Credit cards:* Amex, Diners, Master, Visa. *How to get
there:* Guests can be met at Heathrow Airport or at the Kemble railway station. Bibury is on A433 between Cirencester and Burford. *Telephone:* (028 574) 337. [T]

Bishops Tachbrook, Warwickshire

MALLORY COURT

For sure so fair a place was never seen
Of all that ever charm's romantic eye.
John Keats, 1818

This superb country house, set in 10 acres of cultivated gardens and velvet lawns, is a haven of peace and beauty. It was built early in this century, and much of the original furniture remains. What has since been added is in keeping with its luxurious setting.

A warm country-house atmosphere prevails. Guests relax on big sofas by an open log fire where afternoon tea or drinks are served. Bedrooms are splendidly comfortable, with little extras such as hair dryers and a selection of books.

The oak-paneled dining room serves classic French cuisine that has earned a star from Michelin. You might choose filet mignon topped with foie gras, truffles, and Madeira sauce, or calf's liver with wine, cream, and mustard sauce. The wine list is extensive. Fine china, silver, and crystal enhance the flawless service.

In any contest to choose England's best country-house hotels, Mallory Court would receive high marks.

Proprietors: Jeremy Mort and Alan Holland. *Recreational facilities:* Outdoor pool, tennis, and squash at the hotel; golf and riding nearby. *Other facilities:* Drawing room, garden, laundry-valet service. *Rooms:* 8 with bath, telephone, and TV; 1 suite. Not suitable for children under 12. Very expensive. *Restaurant service:* Luncheon and dinner. *Credit cards:* Amex, Master, Visa. *How to get there:* From Bishops Tachbrook, take Route A452 toward Leamington Spa, which is 2 miles away. Turn right onto Harbury Lane. Mallory Court is on the right. *Telephone:* (0926) 30214. *Agent in the United States:* David Mitchell.[T]

Blanchland, Durham

LORD CREWE ARMS

> On a sudden in the midst of men and day,
> And while I walk'd and talk'd as heretofore,
> I seem'd to move among a world of ghosts,
> And feel myself the shadow of a dream.
> *Alfred, Lord Tennyson*

If walls could talk, the yard-thick walls of the Lord Crewe Arms could tell swashbuckling tales of its turbulent past. It was part of an eleventh-century abbey, home of the White Monks until their massacre by raiders from the north. Centuries later, Tom Forster, a leading figure in the Jacobite rebellion, was hidden in the priest's hiding hole by his sister, Dorothy. On your way to today's Crypt Bar, through stone-flagged rooms and narrow passages, you will walk by this hiding hole in a vast chimney. History comes alive as you gaze into it and ponder the lives of the desperate fugitives who hid there. Dorothy haunts the hotel to this day.

On the cobbled market square of this village set amid heather-covered moors, the local hunt meets before the door of the hotel. A coal fire in a massive stone fireplace, with inglenook, greets the entering guest. Furnished with antiques from many periods, the Lord Crewe Arms is a fine place for history buffs who like to experience their history in comfort.

If you don't stay overnight, try to come by for morning coffee, afternoon tea, or a snack lunch served in the garden. Few inns have quite the ancient atmosphere of the Lord Crewe Arms.

Proprietors: Mr. and Mrs. Gingell and Mr. Todd. *Recreational facilities:* Sailboat rental a short drive away. *Other facilities:* TV lounge, cocktail bar, public bar, garden. *Rooms:* 15 with bath, telephone, and tea-making. Off-season rates; children under 13 free sharing, reduction if in separate room. Moderate. *Restaurant service:* Early and late snacks, tea, dinner. *Credit cards:* Amex, Diners, Master, Visa. *How to get there:* Blanchland is 6 miles from Route A68 on the road to Stanhope. *Telephone:* (043 475) 251.   [T]

Blawith, Cumbria

APPLETREE HOLME FARM

> This little unsuspected Paradise where all is peace.
>   *Thomas Gray,* 1757

One of the smallest gems in Britain is this lodging of extraordinary enchantment. Roy and Shirley Carlsen, having developed their last hotel into one of the most successful country houses in Britain, chose to exchange it for a farmhouse way out on the fells. They enjoy entertaining guests, which is why they entered the hotel business, but as their enterprise grew they found they had little time to spend with visitors. "We love being back to doing everything ourselves," said Shirley. "The nicest kind of people stay at small guest houses, and here we have time to talk to them."

The exterior of the simple farmhouse gives no hint of the luxury and taste within—antiques, oak timbers, beautiful ornaments, big open fires, a wall of books, pictures and flowers everywhere. One bedroom is in a separate cottage called Down House, next to the main house, with an outstanding view, a private patio, and one of the most glamorous bathrooms you are ever likely to come across. Another glamorous bathroom in the main house, with a double bubble bath, was such an unexpected find that it caused us to laugh with delight. Shirley chuckled as she watched us. "We don't warn anyone," she told us, "It's such fun to see their surprise."

All bookings accepted include dinner, and the cooking is as special as the house. Whenever possible they serve food produced on their own or neighboring farms. They bake their own bread and personally select meat, fish, and game. Besides the house guests, they'll serve only one party of up to six dinner guests.

Close by is a luxurious spa. Guests at Appletree can enjoy free use of the pool, whirlpool, and water exercise classes. Other facilities— sauna, squash, exercise classes, hair-dressing salon—are available for a charge. If you can manage it, plan to stay here for a week; just think how welcome those fires would feel in autumn after a hike across the fells.

Proprietors: Roy and Shirley Carlsen. *Closed:* Christmas through January 1. *Recreational facilities:* Lake swimming, riding, and rough shooting a short walk away; hunting, ocean swimming, game, coarse and sea fishing, boat rental, boat trip. *Other facilities:* Lounge, TV lounge, garden. *Rooms:* 4 with bath and tea-making. 2-night minimum advance reservation. Discount for children sharing. Moderate. *Restaurant service:* Dinner by reservation. *How to get there:* In Blawith, which is on Route A5084 just south of Coniston Water (a large lake), turn into a lane directly opposite the Saint John Baptist Church. After almost half a mile, take the first right. Follow this lane to the first left, where the farm is signposted. If you have any problem finding the farm, ask directions at the post office in Blawith. Guests can be met at the Ulverston railway station. *Telephone:* (022 985) 618.

Blockley, Gloucestershire

LOWER BROOK HOUSE

> Every antique farm house and moss-grown cottage is a picture.
>
> *Washington Irving*

This is the sort of place Washington Irving described, now a cozy hotel in a lovely village off the main path of the tourist throngs. When we stopped in one morning, there was a fire burning gently in a vast inglenook fireplace bearing the date 1655; beside it was an enormous foot-operated bellows. The proprietor, Ewan Wright, supervises the traditional English-style cooking and cares about the quality of the food served in the flagstoned dining room. Desserts are all homemade.

The whole of this small inn shines with loving care. Black beams are imbedded in the white plaster walls, decked with hunting horns of copper and brass. Smallish bedrooms, with excellent bathrooms, all have views over the garden. On the third floor you'll slumber under ancient beams, but the bedrooms on the second are a bit larger. In summer, sip your drink beside a murmuring brook in the terraced garden of this happy blend of old and new.

Proprietor: Ewan Wright. *Closed:* January. *Recreational facilities:* Riding, hunting, squash, and golf a short drive away. *Other facilities:* Lounge, cocktail bar, living room, garden. *Rooms:* 8 with bath and TV. 3-day reduction; winter breaks; Christmas program. Moderate. *Restaurant service:* Luncheon, tea, dinner. *Credit cards:* Diners, Master. *How to get there:* Blockley is on Route B4479, which runs from A44 between Moreton-in-Marsh and Broadway. *Telephone:* (0386) 700286.

HARROP FOLD FARM

> Have you become a farmer? Is it not pleasanter than to be shut up within 4 walls and delving eternally with a pen? . . . If you are half as much delighted with the farm as I am, you bless your stars.
>
> *Thomas Jefferson*

Homespun friendliness is the rule at this seventeenth-century Lancashire Longhouse that has been featured as a farm guest house on the BBC and in *Lancashire Life* magazine. Many antiques are used in furnishings and accessories, but there are modern touches too. A tiny cattle barn called the Saetr, an old Norse word, was converted into two bedrooms, each with bathroom, and is decorated in Scandinavian style.

Cooking by son Andrew, a trained chef, emphasizes traditional English country recipes made with local produce. Dinner begins with soup—pea and ham, asparagus, cream of nettle—and continues with an appetizer, main course, dessert, cheese, and fruit, followed by coffee and mints in the lounge. Entrées might include roast turkey, crown roast of lamb, duckling with sage and onion stuffing, or game in season. There is a selection of sweets from the buffet: perhaps apple pie, bilberry tart, and syllabub trifle.

Breakfast prepares you for a day spent walking the fells (a telephone call will bring someone to pick you up if you get too tired to hike back). A buffet of fruits, juices, and cereals is followed by bacon, eggs, sausage, tomatoes, mushrooms, toast, croissants, honey, and home-made marmalade. The Woods have put together a booklet for less energetic types to guide them to Yorkshire dales or Cumbrian lakes and to antique shops, craftsmen, auctions, art galleries, and pubs.

Proprietors: Peter and Victoria Wood. *Recreational facilities:* Riding, hunting, tennis, squash, and indoor pool a short drive away. *Other facilities:* Lounge, TV lounge, cocktail bar, garden. *Rooms:* 7 with bath, TV and tea-making. 2-day reduction. 4-day Christmas program. Not suitable for children. Inexpensive. *Restaurant service:* Dinner. *How to get there:* Do not go into the village of Bolton-by-Bowland. Find Harrop Fold signposted on the road between Grindleton and Slaidburn, somewhat nearer Grindleton. *Telephone:* (02007) 600.

Bonchurch, Isle of Wight

WINTERBOURNE HOTEL

My dear Kate,
  I have taken a most delightful house . . . at Bonchurch—cool, airy, private bathing, everything delicious—I think it is the prettiest place I ever saw in
my life. . . .
  The man with the post bag is swearing in the
passage.   Ever affectionately,
                                        C.D.

> A water fall on the grounds which I have arranged with a carpenter to convert into a perpetual shower bath.
>
> *Charles Dickens,* 1849

A photostat of the original of the letter quoted above is framed at Winterbourne. The waterfall is still in the garden, and a zigzag path descends the cliffs to the beach, where we bought sandwiches made from freshly steamed crab. There are glorious ocean views from the garden terrace and from some bedrooms, all named for Dicken's characters—Peggotty, Trot, Micawber, and so forth. Here the famous author wrote *David Copperfield*. Very much a family man, he had been searching for a rental in a healthy climate for his "chickens."

This lovely house is very well furnished and quite luxurious, with fine modern bathrooms. Guests mix easily here. The Isle of Wight is beautiful and worth the trip. Bonchurch has more than once won an award as the "Best Kept Village."

Proprietors: Pat and Terry O'Connor. *Closed:* January and February. *Recreational facilities:* Outdoor pool and ocean swimming at the hotel; golf, tennis, squash, fishing, boat rental, boat trips, deep-sea fishing, and riding a short drive away. *Other facilities:* Drawing room, TV lounge, cocktail bar, garden. *Rooms:* 19 with bath and TV. No children under 5; reduction for children sharing. Expensive. *Restaurant service:* Snacks, tea, and dinner. *Credit cards:* Amex, Diners, Master, Visa. *How to get there:* Ferries run to the Isle of Wight from Lymington, Portsmouth, and Southampton, which can all be reached by train from Waterloo Station, London. A reservation well ahead for an auto is essential weekends and all summer. There are local buses for transportation on the island, and cars can be rented there. *Telephone:* (0983) 852535.

MILLSTREAM HOTEL

Bosham, my good Herbert,
Thy birthplace—the sea-creek—the petty rill
That falls into it—the green field—the grey
church.

Alfred, Lord Tennyson, 1849

Although the Millstream's roots date from 1701, when it was a malt house, it is tastefully decorated in light and airy contemporary colors, and such amenities as modern carpeted bathrooms are strictly twentieth century.

Bosham, favored by yachtsmen and the loveliest village we saw on the south coast of England, offers more than beauty. It was probably the English headquarters of King Canute, the Dane who conquered England in 1016. His little daughter is thought to be buried in the venerable church that still survives, one of the very few Saxon churches remaining in Britain. Harold, the last Saxon king of England—killed by William's army at that famous battle in 1066—had a manor here. From the Millstream in Bosham center, walk to the waterfront street, where any auto left parked too long is completely covered when the unusually high tide floods in daily. The cluster of boats in the placid blue harbor may invite you to hire one and try some sailing yourself.

The dining room at the Millstream serves excellent meals, and the attractive bar, furnished with cane, draws visiting yachtsmen. One American told us this was his favorite lodging on a tour throughout England.

Manager: Nicholas and Lesley Barker. *Recreational facilities:* Sailing instruction, boat rental, boat trips, and deep-sea fishing a short walk away; riding a short drive away. *Other facilities:* Lounge, cocktail bar, garden. *Rooms:* 22 with bath, telephone, tea-making, and TV. 2-day reduction. Expensive. *Restaurant service:* Luncheon, tea, dinner. *Credit cards:* Amex, Diners, Master, Visa. *How to get there:* Turn south off Route A27, 4 miles west of Chichester. Guests can be met at the Bosham railway station. *Telephone:* (0243) 573 234. *Agent in the United States:* Best Western. [T]

WILLMEAD FARM

> A Devonshire cottage . . . . crushed beneath its burden
> of thatch . . . it seems to be stationed there for no more
> obvious purpose than to keep a promise to your fancy.
> *Henry James,* 1872

A visit to Willmead Farm captures, if briefly, a moment in the rural past, although it is no longer a working farm. At this charmer you'll find great atmosphere, log fires, and a warm welcome from Hilary Roberts, a widow.

The house dates back to the fourteenth century. One room is a medieval hall with minstrels' gallery. In it is a grandfather clock that towers high into the two-story room. The living room has big comfortable chairs and sofa in front of a massive stone fireplace, decked with gleaming copper and brass. Paintings and blue and white china decorate traditional white plaster walls. Magazines are on antique tables, and shelves hold books. Bring any spirits you might want to sip during an evening.

The dining room is a step down from the living room, open to it and set off by enormous rough beams. Large Chippendale chairs surround a table where guests have breakfast together. For dinner—none served at the house—you can walk along a footpath to a village restaurant or drive a few miles to nearby country-house hotels. A cozy old world awaits you at Willmead Farm.

Proprietor: Hilary Roberts. *Closed:* Christmas and New Year weeks. *Smoking:* Not permitted. *Facilities:* Living room, lounge, garden. *Rooms:* 3 sharing baths. No children under 10. Very inexpensive. *How to get there:* From Bovey Tracey, take Route A382 toward Moretonhampstead. Take the first left past the Hawkmoor Hospital and continue 1/2 mile. *Telephone:* (06477) 214.

Brampton, Cumbria

FARLAM HALL

Thirty feet high is the Wall . . . but the Wall itself
is not more wonderful than the town behind it . . .
a thin town eighty miles long. Think of it! One roaring rioting town. . . . On one side heather, woods and
ruins where Picts hide, and on the other, a vast
town—long like a snake, and wicked like a snake.
Rudyard Kipling, 1906

Close enough to Hadrian's Wall to have been part of the wicked city
described by Kipling above, Farlam Hall is a place to spend a few days

while you explore this lovely rolling farm country that has such a fascinating past. A warm reception greets guests at this country-house hotel for people who like quiet.

The building is listed as of historical and architectural interest (John Wesley is reputed to have preached in the house), and is furnished in keeping. In the lounge there is a tile-faced fireplace, as well as upholstered pieces in cretonne and velvet beside antique tables that hold unusual English magazines. Up a winding stairway are warmly carpeted, well-furnished bedrooms; attention to detail is meticulous. In exceptionally pretty gardens, ducklings swim on a little pond and bluebells grow along a stream with a tiny stone bridge.

Son Barry Quinion offers Cordon Bleu cooking, using only the best of materials prepared with great care. The set menu provides a choice of three entrées, one of which is usually something unusual, such as wood pigeon braised in red wine or saddle of roast hare. Lobster soup or prawn and avocado salad might start the meal. Many residents of the area come in for dinner, chatting with Alan Quinion as he dispenses drinks in the attractive small bar. In an atmosphere well-mannered but not formal, coat and tie are preferred but not requisite.

Proprietors: The Quinion and Stevenson families. *Closed:* February and Christmas. *Recreational facilities:* Lake swimming and riding a short drive away. *Other facilities:* Lounge, cocktail bar, garden. *Rooms:* 13 with bath, telephone, and TV. Ground floor rooms. Winter breaks. *Children:* Under 5 not permitted. Moderate to expensive. *Restaurant service:* Dinner. *Credit cards:* Amex, Master, Visa. *How to get there:* Farlam Hall is on Route A689, 2 1/2 miles east of Brampton, on the road to Alston. *Telephone:* (069 76) 234.

Branscombe, Devon

MASONS ARMS

It beckoned "Come In!" with every breath of air.
Charles Dickens

The lingering associations of an old smugglers' haunt cling to this fourteenth-century inn, for this was the hangout of the Branscombe smugglers, always referred to as the "gentlemen," as in Rudyard Kipling's poem "A Smuggler's Song." Children were taught to ignore sounds of voices in the night or muffled steps of a horse that should have been quiet in its stable.

The word "quaint" could have been coined for the Mason Arms. You may stop for a snack lunch on the lawn, where you will sit under a thatched umbrella that matches the thatched roofs of many of the houses in this captivating village, the property of King Alfred in the ninth century. The South–Sea–Islands look is quite unexpected in England. Some bedrooms are in converted cottages across the road from the ancient inn. This lodging will best suit those who enjoy socializing in a friendly bar. The attractive upstairs lounge seems almost unused, as we have found is frequently true of lounges above the main floor. No other hotel guest came in while we spent an evening reading there.

While here you will be in the stream of English life from long ago to the present, but with all of today's comforts.

Proprietor: Janet Inglis. *Recreational facilities:* Ocean swimming a short walk away; riding a short drive away. *Facilities for children:* Baby-listening. *Other facilities:* Lounge, public bar, garden. *Rooms:* 21 with bath, telephone, and TV; ground-floor rooms. 2-night reduction, Monday–Thursday. Winter breaks; Christmas program. Minimum 2-night advance reservations in season. Inexpensive to expensive. *Restaurant service:* Snacks, tea, dinner. *How to get there:* Take Route A3052 from Lyme Regis west to B3774 to Seaton. From there travel west along the coast to Branscombe. *Telephone:* (029 780) 300.

BROADWAY HOTEL

> Broadway is the very pattern of the old English village
> one sees on the stage.
>
> *Richard Le Gallienne,* 1900

The Broadway will call "Come in" to you. The architecture of the half-timbered, fifteenth-century building, with its two-story beamed and balconied lounge, offers so much atmosphere that you'll forgive the modern furnishings that predominate in the bedrooms. Formerly owned by the Abbots of Pershore, it has a garden where teas are served and a cheerful bar with traditional red carpet, diamond-paned windows, timbered ceiling, and horse brasses decorating the massive chimney beam.

Those who want to take a train out of London for an English country experience will enjoy walks through the streets of this village of golden Cotswold stone. Fine shops for browsing display antiques, quality gifts, clothes, books, and foodstuffs. Day trips to neighboring towns and villages can be made by local bus.

In season Broadway is jammed, and the hotel will not accept advance booking for just one night.

Manager: Mrs. P. Swinden. *Recreational facilities:* Riding a short drive away. *Other facilities:* Lounge, public bar, garden. *Rooms:* 24, 22 with bath, all with telephone, TV, and tea-making. Winter breaks. Christmas program. Moderate to expensive. *Restaurant service:* Luncheon, snacks, tea, dinner. *Credit cards:* Amex, Diners, Master, Visa. *How to get there:* Broadway is southwest of Stratford on Route A46. Guests will be met at the Evesham railway station without charge. *Telephone:* (0386) 852401. [T]

COLLIN HOUSE HOTEL

Take from this hearth its warmth,
From this room its charm,
From this inn its amity,
Return them not, but return.

Anonymous

Warmth, charm, and amity are keynotes at Collin House. The friendly sixteenth-century stone house has been carefully restored to retain its character. We had lunch in a beamed bar, sitting on armchairs grouped around an inglenook fireplace where a log fire burned even in the morning. In a candlelit dining room, walls are hung with original paintings, and mullion windows look out on a garden. The menu is varied, and the food is outstanding.

Well-carpeted bedrooms come with comfortable chairs, shoe-cleaning and sewing kits, and biscuits to nibble on; each has a book made up of information about the area, with brochures and suggestions of things to do. Two have four-poster beds, and those on the third floor are very romantic, heavily raftered, and open to peaked ceilings.

John spends a great deal of time helping guests map out their plans for the day, routing them along the most pleasing country lanes to whatever their interests. If these include antiques and paintings, he will direct guests to the best antique shops and galleries.

The setting is peaceful, in eight acres of garden about a mile away from the crowds that are drawn to the picture-postcard Cotswold village of Broadway. This is a place to spend more than overnight. Just thinking about it has us wishing we could be there tomorrow.

Proprietors: John and Judith Mills. *Closed:* 3 days at Christmas. *Recreational facilities:* Outdoor pool at the hotel; riding, hunting, and golf nearby. *Other facilities:* Lounge, cocktail lounge, garden. *Rooms:* 7 with bath. Winter breaks. Moderate. *Restaurant service:* Luncheon, snacks, and dinner. *Credit cards:* Master, Visa. *How to get there:* Take Route A44 one mile northwest from Broadway. Turn right onto Collin Lane. The hotel is on the right. *Telephone:* (0386) 858354.

LYGON ARMS

> We put up at a most comfortable cleanly house where
> a delicious loyn of veal was ready, and I was ready
> for eating it; which I did in ample quantity, and had
> then a superabundant temptation by an apricot tart.
> *John Byng,* 1787

Thus did the author describe the Lygon Arms. Its exact age is unknown, but much of it was built by men who were alive two hundred years before the Mayflower sailed for America. The year of that voyage, 1620, is carved over the main entrance, added when the old coaching inn was enlarged. It is carved also in the headboard of a four-poster in one of the old chambers used today.

There are two modern wings in the extensive rear garden, but if you want to slip into another century you will ask to lodge in the inn's medieval section, where some bedrooms have walls 4 feet thick, some have fireplaces, and all are furnished with antiques. A silk-hosed gallant in powdered wig would feel right at home—that is, until he opened the door to the luxurious adjoining bathroom.

Legend has it that Oliver Cromwell slept here just before the Battle of Worcester in 1651. The inn has played host to Charles I and, much more recently, to the present duke of Edinburgh. The antiques in the public rooms are treasures, especially two tables, one from the seventeenth century and one Elizabethan, both featured in *The Dictionary of English Furniture.*

There is a four-day Christmas celebration, when carols are sung by candlelight in the galleried Great Hall and guests join for hot toddy and mince pies after midnight mass in the village. In addition to the traditional Christmas dinner, there are two black-tie dinners, Christmas games, and teas.

The Lygon Arms, possibly the most famous country inn in Britain, lives on graciously from one long continuous past into the bustling present, a hotel full of smartly dressed people who demand the most modern luxuries while enjoying English history.

Manager: Kirk Ritchie *Recreational facilities:* Tennis at the hotel; riding, hunting, squash, and golf a short drive away. *Other facilities:* Lounges, TV lounge, cocktail bar, public bar, garden, gift shop. *Rooms:* 58 with bath, TV, and telephone; 5 suites. Suitable for wheelchair guests. 2-day reduction; Christmas program. Very expensive. *Restaurant service:* Luncheon, early and late snacks, tea, dinner. *Credit cards:* Amex, Carte Blanche, Diners, Master, Visa. *How to get there:* Broadway is southwest of Stratford on Route A46. Take a bus from Waterloo Station, London, to Broadway, or a train from Paddington Station to Moreton-in-Marsh. Car rental available locally. *Telephone:* (0386) 852 255. *Agent in the United States:* Scott Calder.[T]

BAY TREE

O Fair is Moreton in the Marsh
And Stow on the wide wold
But fairer far is Burford town
With its stone roofs grey and old

H.C. Beeching

This was the home of Sir Laurence Tanfield, the unpopular lord chief baron of the Exchequer for Elizabeth I, so it's likely that she visited the Bay Tree when she was in Burford in 1574. The past lives everywhere around you at this inn. Oak paneling, enormous log-burning fireplaces, and a minstrel's gallery are but a few of the architectural delights. The house is built around a miniature courtyard, and behind it lies a garden with sun loggia, stone terraces, and a lily pond. A little bar is tucked under the stairs, and there is a library for quiet browsing.

As you stroll along the wide High Street, which leads down to the River Windrush, you'll see handsome houses built when the town flourished with the wool trade. The architecture is different from that of most Cotswold towns—half-timbering on brown stone—as there was wood available from the Forest of Wychwood. You may begin to imagine yourself on a stage set and think you hear coaches and horses clattering along the cobblestones.

Proprietors: The King Family. *Closed:* December 25 and 26. *Recreational facilities:* Golf a short walk away. *Other facilities:* 3 lounges, library, cocktail bar, conservatory, garden. *Rooms:* 20 with bath, telephone, and TV; 2 suites. 3-day reduction; winter breaks November through April; reduction for children under 12 sharing. Moderate. *Restaurant service:* Luncheon, snacks, tea, dinner. *How to get there:* Burford is on Route A361 between Chipping Norton and Swindon. Trains can be met at the Charlbury station. Bus from Victoria Station, London, almost to the hotel door; get off on High Street, at corner of Sheep Street. Car rental available locally. *Telephone:* (099 382) 3137.

RED LION HOTEL

> Happier life I cannot imagine than this vagrancy . . . and towards evening a courteous welcome in a rustic inn.
>
> *Thomas De Quincy,* 1807

In a picturesque moorland village with a maypole on its village green, the Red Lion stands on the bank of the River Wharfe. A village church-yard has Viking gravestones, and the famous Bolton Abbey is near-by. This plain, well-run little inn, with a friendly staff and a garden, might be a convenient stopover for those driving gypsy style, without advance reservations.

Although Burnsall is a peaceful place during the week, we'd avoid it on a weekend, when it's mobbed with holiday-makers from the cities to the south and when families crowd the Red Lion at noon to enjoy its traditional Sunday roast-beef dinner.

Proprietor: Mrs. Pat Warnett. *Facilities:* Lounge, TV lounge, public bar, garden. *Rooms:* 12, 3 with bath. 2-day reduction; 2-day winter breaks; reduction for children under 13 sharing. Inexpensive. *Restaurant service:* Snacks and dinner. *How to get there:* Burnsall is on Rt. B6160, north of Bolton Abbey. *Telephone:* (075 672) 204.

ANGEL HOTEL

"And this," said Mr. Pickwick, looking up, "is the
Angel!" We alight here, Sam."
Charles Dickens, 1837

Dickens had quite an affection for "the bright little town of Bury St
Edmunds." He visited the Angel Hotel twice to give readings, and you
can stay today in the "fine room" where he slept, preserved, with a
four-poster bed, as it was more than a century ago. In *The Pickwick
Papers* he immortalized the Angel as the place where Sam Weller first
ran into Job Trotter.

The hotel's two dining rooms, one in a medieval vaulted cellar, are
recommended in English food guides. Roast beef from a huge joint,
rolled to your table and kept warm under a big silver dome, is carved
to your order. The wine list is above average.

Town records first mention the Angel as an inn in 1452. Most of
the present ivy-covered building dates from 1779. This busy hotel looks
across the road at the massive gate to public gardens that surround
romantic ruins of an eleventh-century abbey founded by King Canute.
The historic market town is a fine place for a train traveler, as there
is so much to see here.

Proprietors: Mary Gough. *Recreational facilities:* Tennis, indoor
pool, squash, sauna, and riding nearby. *Facilities for children:* Baby-listening. *Other facilities:* Lounge, cocktail bar. *Rooms:* 40 with bath,
telephone, and TV. Weekend breaks. Expensive. *Restaurant service:*
Luncheon, snacks, tea, dinner. *Credit cards:* Amex, Diners, Master,
Visa. *How to get there:* The town can be reached by train and bus
(coach). *Telephone:* (0284) 753921. *Agent in the United States:* Josephine Barr.   [T]

Canterbury, Kent

FALSTAFF HOTEL

> from every shires ende
> of Engelond, to Caunterbury they wende,
> The holy blisful martir for to seke.
>
> *Geoffrey Chaucer,* 1388

The Falstaff Hotel had not yet been built when Chaucer told tales of the pilgrims he brought together to wend their way from London to Canterbury. At that time the gates of the town were locked as darkness fell. Those who arrived late, perhaps from much feasting and story-telling along the way, had to lie under the walls of the medieval town until morning. In 1403, the Falstaff went up just outside the Westgate to house such laggards. Today it is part of central Canterbury and a short walk from the cathedral.

The character that for centuries has attracted the traveler is em-phasized by the inn's black and white timbered upper stories that overhang the street, its mullioned windows, and its early paneling and heavy beams secured by wooden pegs. One room has a four-poster, but others have unit furniture and good modern bathrooms. Public rooms are properly atmospheric but rather impersonal, to be expected in a town as bustling as Canterbury. The dining room is busy, serving locals and tourists alike. It was intriguing to learn that the word "can-ter" derives from a description of the easy lope of the horses the pil-grims rode across the downs on their way to Canterbury.

Manager: Rolf Steinmetz. *Facilities:* Lounge, public bar, parking. *Rooms:* 24 with bath, TV, telephone, and tea-making. Weekend breaks all year. Moderate. *Restaurant service:* Luncheon, snacks, dinner. *Credit cards:* Amex, Diners, Visa. *How to get there:* The hotel is on St. Dunstan's Street. Take train from Charing Cross station, London, to Canterbury West Station, which is 400 yards from the hotel. *Telephone:* (0227) 462138.

AYNSOME MANOR

Hospitality without formality
With heartiness and cordiality.

Anonymous

Decorated with antiques and charm, the old manor is far more beautiful inside than its rather severe exterior might lead you to expect. The remarkable freestanding spiral staircase of stone, genuine Adam, is a beauty, as are the Adam fireplace and elaborately molded Adam ceiling.

This is an ideal spot for the single traveler, especially one who does not care to drive alone. The owners, the Varleys, will not only meet guests at the train but will cart them around while they go about their daily errands. Anyone is welcome to jump into the car wherever they go. Tony Varley and his head chef were recently filmed at Aynsome Manor by the BBC for an international-cooking series. A single room is just half the price of a double.

Proprietors: The Varley family. *Closed:* January 2–22. *Recreational facilities:* Indoor pool, outdoor saltwater pool, ocean and lake swimming, tennis, riding, golf, and trout fishing a short drive away. *Other facilities:* 2 lounges, cocktail bar, garden. *Rooms:* 13 with bath, telephone, TV, and tea-making. 3-day reduction; reduction for children sharing; winter breaks; Christmas program. Expensive. *Restaurant service (no smoking):* Dinner. *Credit cards:* Amex, Master, Visa. *How to get there:* Take Route A590 to signs for Cartmel. The hotel is north of the village center. Guests can be met at the Grange-over-Sands railway station. *Telephone:* (044 854) 36653. [T]

Chagford, Devon

GIDLEIGH PARK

There are wastes and wilds, crags of granite, views into far-off districts, and the sound of waters hurrying away over their rocky beds, enough to satisfy the largest hungering and thirsting after poetical delight. I shall never forget the feelings of delicious entrancement with which I approached the outskirts of Dartmoor.

William Howitt, 1841

Gidleigh Park is one of the most peaceful and secluded hotels in Britain. Set 700 feet high on the edge of Dartmoor, in wastes and wilds and crags of granite, protected on three sides and offering magnificent views on the fourth, it is a mile and a half up a very narrow lane from the nearest road. Terraced gardens step down to the Teign River, which you can hear in the night as it hurries away over its rocky bed.

Paul and Kay Henderson are Americans, Kay from Indiana, Paul brought up in a military family that moved around the country. They met while at Purdue University. When a job took them to London in 1970, they spent vacations visiting Michelin 3-star restaurants and staying in the best small English country hotels. Kay went to Cordon Bleu classes in London and Paris and taught a cooking class in her London home.

When they bought Gidleigh Park in 1977, their aim was to develop a perfect country inn with "English country-house atmosphere, French food, and American plumbing." That they soon succeeded is attested by the awards and accolades showered on them by food guides, wine associations, and European publications. The *American Wine Spectator* gave Gidleigh Park a "Grand Award" for having the best wine list in Britain. More significant, perhaps, is that over half the guests are returnees.

The mansion was built by a shipping magnate in 1928 as a country retreat. Oak-paneled public rooms are furnished with antiques, comfortable seating, deep-piled carpets, and fresh flowers. Fires burn winter and summer. Bedrooms, some with balconies, rate high on comfort. The Hendersons are welcoming and mix with their guests. Relaxed informality is the rule.

Besides the wonderful food and wine, you'll find "character, courtesy, calm, comfort," the attributes that made Gidleigh Park qualify to join the prestigious Relais et Chateaux association.

Proprietors: Kay and Paul Henderson. *Recreational facilities:* Tennis at the hotel; river swimming (for the daring), riding, golf, and windsurfing nearby. *Facilities for children:* Baby-sitting. *Other facilities:* Hall lounge, drawing room, cocktail bar, garden. *Rooms:* 12 with bath, telephone, and TV. Winter breaks. No children under 12 except infants. Expensive to very expensive. *Restaurant service:* Luncheon, snacks, tea, and dinner. *Credit cards:* Amex, Diners, Master, Visa. *How to get there:* From Chagford Square, face Webbers, with Lloyds Bank on your right. Turn right into Mill Street. After 200 yards, turn to the right and go downhill to Factory Crossroad. Go straight across into Holy Street and follow the lane 1 1/2 miles to the end. Do not go into Gidleigh. *Telephone:* (06473) 2367. [T]

MILL END HOTEL

Wild Dartmoor! thou that midst thy mountains rude
Hast robed thyself with haughty solitude.

Felicia Hemans

The Mill End Hotel is a converted old mill, a fine example of adaptive preservation. Afternoon tea in the lounge, a cheerful blaze of wood fire on the hearth, is a charming English experience. Soft chairs and couches are slipcovered in flowered English linen; tables hold fresh flowers and copies of *Country Life;* a chess board is set up ready for play. When it's time for a drink before dinner, there is a brass gong to strike for service. After the first ''bong,'' guests come drifting in, and everyone talks to everyone else.

Unusual dishes on the menu merit comment. Hors d'oeuvres might be finnan haddock in cheese sauce or fresh tomato mousse before a main course of roast pheasant, guinea fowl, or beef burgundy pie. Then the sweets trolley rolls up laden with Sacher torte, gooseberry gateau, lemon soufflé—"and wouldn't you like to try some of each, Madam?" A cheese trolley rivals the sweets trolley in popularity.

The third-floor bedrooms have beams, the more modern ones on the ground floor have individual terraces. Colorful chairs on the lawn invite lounging where rooks circle over the sun-dappled river. All of this loveliness is in Dartmoor National Park. You can travel far over its rugged, lonely moors and meet only sheep and wild ponies.

Proprietor: Nicholas Craddock. *Closed:* Late December; open for New Year's Eve. *Recreational facilities:* River swimming at the hotel; outdoor pool a short walk away; tennis, hunting, and indoor and outdoor riding a short drive away. *Facilities for children:* Children's supper. *Other facilities:* Drawing room, lounge, cocktail bar, garden. *Rooms:* 17 with bath, TV, and telephone. Ground-floor rooms. Off-season rates; children under 15 free if sharing, 10% discount if in separate room. Moderate. *Restaurant service:* Luncheon, tea, dinner. *Credit cards:* Amex, Diners, Master, Visa. *How to get there:* Take Route A30 from Exeter to A382. Find Mill End signposted on A382. Do not turn into the village of Chagford. *Telephone:* (06473) 2282.

THORNWORTHY HOUSE

But here O here in Devon, listen long,
To England's own deep song.

Alfred Noyes, 1927

High in Dartmoor National Park, this rather sophisticated guest house is a Victorian home set in two acres of garden with a duck pond. Its windows offer dramatic views over moor and vale. Wild rhododendron abounds.

Philip and Vicky Jevons prefer their visitors to feel like house guests, not hotel clients. Philip recently retired as a commodities broker with Shearson Lehman Brothers in London. Vicky is an American, but is a long-time resident of England.

The atmosphere is informal and relaxed. Before dinner, which is country-style, people gather in the living room. Some fruits and vegetables are from Thornworthy's garden, and the famed Devon clotted cream is from a neighbor's farm. Homemade ice cream is Vicky's specialty. The wine list is varied and reasonable.

The Jevons redecorated when they took over the guest house, so everything is fresh and very attractive, with magazines and good books for browsing. A walk across the surrounding wild moorland makes a fine contrast to the warmth of Thornworthy House.

Proprietors: Philip and Vicky Jevons. *Recreational facilities:* Tennis at the house; riding, and fly fishing nearby. *Facilities for children:* Baby-sitting. *Other facilities:* Living room, garden room, garden. *Rooms:* 5 doubles with bath; 2 singles sharing bath; self-catering 3-bedroom cottage. Moderate. *Credit cards:* Amex, Diners, Master, Visa. *How to get there:* From Chagford Square, turn right into Mill Street. After 150 yards, fork left at the sign to Kestor Rock. At top of Waye Hill, the road curves to the left. Immediately after, take the right turn signposted to Thornworthy. *Telephone:* (06473) 3297.

Cheltenham, Gloucestershire

HOTEL DE LA BERE

. . . the large and spacious houses, with their oriel, latticed windows, their huge fireplaces and their gabled roofs, breathe of the days of hose and doublet, of pearl-embroidered stomachers, and complicated oaths.
Jerome K. Jerome, 1889

This manor was already old when Shakespeare was born not far away. Its great hall and minstrel gallery probably echoed to the performance of his plays, acted by the strolling players who performed at inns and manor houses as was the custom of the time. Today it is a rare combination of ancient house and fine sporting facilities that will be enjoyed by those who like to keep active as they tour. Within its stone walls and on its sweeping lawns, with their magnificent old trees and formal gardens, are four tennis courts, five squash courts, a large outdoor swimming pool, and a pitch-and-putt golf course.

The house was built at the time of the Wars of the Roses. Its spacious bedrooms, some crossbeamed with high slanting ceilings, others with four-poster beds (and also some with modern furniture), are named for English kings and queens, some of whom probably slept in them. Rare oak paneling, ornate plasterwork, open fires in huge hearths, and massive timberwork evoke the pageantry of Tudor days. Cuisine is first-class, with a good wine selection in all price ranges.

The Regency town of Cheltenham has fine shopping, outdoor cafés, and antique stores set along wide promenades. The hotel overlooks the Cheltenham racecourse. For those who like to get in a daily game or swim, this unique hotel is a good center for such attractions as Bath, Stratford, Oxford, and the romantic Cotswold villages.

Manager: Robert Rizzo. *Recreational facilities:* Tennis, squash, outdoor pool, pitch-and-putt golf course, indoor tennis and badminton, sauna, and gymnasium at the hotel; riding nearby. *Facilities for children:* baby-listening; children's meals. *Other facilities:* Several lounges, cocktail bar, public bar, garden. *Rooms:* 60 with bath, TV, telephone, and tea-making. 2-day reduction; discount for children sharing (under 3 free); Christmas and New Year's program. Expensive. *Restaurant service:* Luncheon, snacks, tea, dinner. *Credit cards:* Amex, Diners, Master, Visa. *How to get there:* The hotel is on A46, 2 miles northeast of Cheltenham in Southam village. *Telephone:* (0242) 37771. *Agents in the United States:* THF. [T]

Chipping Campden, Gloucestershire

KINGS ARMS

> And there is Chipping Campden . . . which fortunately
> is still a real little town and not simply a show place
> and glorified tea establishment for tourists. There is
> no Ye Olde Chipping Campden nonsense about it.
> *J. B. Priestley,* 1934

This Georgian hotel stands in the square by the medieval covered outdoor market hall on what historian Sir George Trevelyan called the
"most beautiful village street in England." The house is handsome,
with friendly service. Oriental rugs on polished floors lead to an attractive old bar and beyond it to a garden. Fresh flowers and fruit in the
bedrooms, furnished to reflect the period, add to the feeling of gracious
hospitality.

The dining room receives rosettes in English food guides and offers an unusual service—late suppers for those who want to attend the
Shakespeare plays in Stratford, only 12 miles away. Chipping Campden is one of the most beautiful of the Cotswold villages, and the Kings
Arms is so agreeable that you may want to make it your center for a
long visit.

Manager: Linda Graham. *Recreational facilities:* Riding, golf, and
tennis nearby. *Other facilities:* Lounge, cocktail bar, garden. *Rooms:*
14, 2 with bath. 3-day reduction; winter breaks; Christmas program.
Inexpensive to moderate. *Restaurant service:* Snacks, dinner. *Credit
cards:* Master, Visa. *How to get there:* Chipping Campden is on Route
B4081, which runs off A44 between Broadway and Moreton-in-Marsh.
Telephone: (0386) 840 256.   [T]

Climping, West Sussex

BAILIFFSCOURT HOTEL

I know not how it is with you—
I love the first and last,
The whole field of the present view,
The whole flow of the past.

Robert Louis Stevenson, 1883

This medieval-looking house was built just over a half century ago, at tremendous cost, to satisfy a whim of Lord Moyne's. On a thousand-acre estate bordering the sea, he found a moat surrounding the site of a courthouse tended by bailiff monks in the twelfth century. To restore this bailiffs' court, Britain was scoured for features from ancient buildings: a molded oaken ceiling from a rectory, ceiling beams from a barn, an ancient door with its original lock and hinge from a stable, medieval windows rescued from deserted abbeys and manors. Stones and timbers from the original courthouse were found embedded in derelict farm buildings on the estate. Arches, doorways, quoins, and windows were carefully restored for the new building, four-sided around a square courtyard. Architecturally correct, Bailiffscourt is one of the most beautiful and expensive fakes in the world.

Since 1948 it has been a romantic luxury hotel. Eight bedrooms have four-posters with floral hangings; nine have working fireplaces. Medieval wooden furniture is combined with comfortable tapestry and velvet-covered chairs and sofas. Bathrooms, however, are luxuriously twentieth century.

In summer a cold buffet luncheon may be enjoyed in a rose-clad courtyard or a walled garden. Christmas at Bailiffscourt evokes "merrie olde England," with mulled wine before log fires in great stone fireplaces and parties under rough-hewn oaken beams. New Year's brings another festive program.

Manager: Tim Lamming. *Recreational facilities:* Ocean swimming, outdoor pool, tennis, sauna, and exercise room at the hotel; riding, sailing, and windsurfing nearby. *Other facilities:* Lounge, cocktail bar, garden, helicopter landing pad. *Rooms:* 20 with bath, TV, and telephone; 2 self-catering cottages. Midweek reduction. Breaks. No children under 8. Expensive to very expensive. *Restaurant service:* Luncheon, tea, dinner. *Credit cards:* Amex, Diners, Master, Visa. *How to get there:* Take Route A284 from just south of Arundel. Turn right onto Route A259. The hotel is on the first road to the left, near Littlehampton. *Telephone:* (0903) 723511. *Agent in the United States:* Ray Morrow.   [T]

Constantine Bay, Cornwall

TREGLOS HOTEL

> The restless Atlantic is ever thundering on this iron-walled coast.
>
> *Sabine Baring-Gould,* 1876

From our bedroom window we watched the Atlantic thunder on this coast. We enjoyed feeling snug while the wind howled outside, drifting to sleep with the sound of the waves and the smell of the sea.

This well-kept seaside hotel, not at all quaint but very pleasant, is set well back from the ocean on an unspoiled part of the busy Cornwall coast, away from the summer crowds at the seaside resort towns. The building is late nineteenth-century with later additions. Furnishings in the sunny public rooms seem to have evolved over the years without any help from decorators. The effect is cheerful and friendly, especially when fires are lit. Plain bedrooms in light colors have unit furniture—ask for one facing the sea. Bed boards are available, and your shoes will be polished if you leave them outside your door. The staff is friendly and solicitous, influenced, no doubt, by the caring attitude of the owners, Ted and Barbara Barlow.

If you are traveling with teen-agers, they'd welcome a few days here to enjoy all the sporting facilities. Younger children are well provided for, too. Most of the guests seem to be English, who come to golf, to walk along cliff paths rich in smuggling history and now protected by the National Trust, and to bask on sun lounges on protected terraces in the garden. Many are returnees, always a good sign.

Proprietors: Barbara and Ted Barlow. *Closed:* November to mid-March. *Recreational facilities:* Indoor pool, ocean swimming, surfing, boat trips, tennis, and Jacuzzi at the hotel; riding, boat rental, water-skiing, and fishing for mackerel, bass, pollack, and shark nearby. *Facilities for children:* Baby-sitting and -listening, games room, and children's meals. *Other facilities:* 2 lounges, card room, snooker room, cocktail bar, laundry facilities, sun terrace, garden. *Rooms:* 44 with bath, telephone, and TV; 4 self-catering flats. Suitable for wheel-chair guests. Off-season rates. Expensive. *Restaurant service:* Luncheon, snacks, tea, dinner (coat and tie). *How to get there:* Constantine Bay is signposted on the coast road, Route B3276, between Padstow and Newquay. *Telephone:* (0841) 520727.　　　　　　　　　　　　[T]

Cornhill-on-Tweed, Northumberland

TILLMOUTH PARK

> From Flodden ridge
> The Scots beheld the English host
> Leave Barmoor Wood, their evening post
> And heedful watched them as they crossed
> The Till by Twizel Bridge.
>
> *Sir Walter Scott*

The map of the border region between England and Scotland contains many crossed swords denoting ancient battlefields and shows the strongholds from which the border lords once made their sorties. It was across Twizel Bridge, on the Tillmouth Park estate, that Lord Surrey led the English artillery on the fateful morning of the Battle of Flodden in 1513.

At the mouth of the Till on the English bank of the River Tweed, which defines the border with Scotland, is this magnificent Victorian mansion surrounded by a 1,000-acre estate. The entrance hall is impressive—oak balcony, stained glass, framed tapestries, and a 43-pound mounted salmon caught by Lady Burnet, the nonresident owner of Tillmouth Park. The galleried drawing room, with a massive stone fireplace and deep armchairs, would make a fine setting for an Agatha Christie mystery. It's easy to picture Hercule Poirot gathering all the guests at a house party together for questioning here. The Sir Walter Scott bedroom is magnificent, and all are spacious, with memories of more formal days. One has a four-poster.

Velvety lawns surround the hotel. Salmon leap in the rivers Till and Tweed, which flow through the estate, with fishing rights controlled by the hotel. Guests should book in advance to reserve a boat or ghillie to go after salmon or sea trout, but the manager can usually arrange for brown trout or coarse fishing at short notice.

Northumberland is a beautiful county of prosperous farmland, less well known to Americans than many parts of England. It is a pleasure to drive through it and end the day at distinguished Tillmouth Park.

Manager: Richard Davis. *Recreational facilities:* Fishing and river swimming at the hotel; tennis, riding, and hunting a short drive away. *Facilities for children:* Baby-sitting and -listening. *Other facilities:* Drawing room, cocktail bar, garden. *Rooms:* 13 with bath, telephone, TV, and tea-making. 2-night reduction; breaks. New Year's program; reduction for children. Moderate to expensive. *Restaurant service:* Luncheon, early and late snacks, dinner. *Credit cards:* Amex, Diners, Master, Visa. *How to get there:* Cornhill-on-Tweed is on Route A697 between Coldstream and Crookham. From the village center take A698 to Tillmouth Park. *Telephone:* (0890) 2255.   [T]

Coxwold, North Yorkshire

FAUCONBERG ARMS

Coxwold . . . is really a show village, a picture of mellowness and grace with a fine inn, the Fauconberg Arms.

James Herriot, 1979

A more attractive little inn would be hard to find: traditional white walls, red rugs, heavy black beams, a wealth of old blue and white china, a Welsh dresser loaded with antiques. Add to this a setting in an enchanting village, a warm welcome, a friendly atmosphere, and first-class cuisine. Who could ask for more?

Bedrooms are prettily done up with matching wallpapers, spreads, and sheets by Sanderson. Even the ceilings are papered, and all is spotlessly maintained. The largest bedroom has a shower built into one corner.

Silvery stone houses line the broad street of Coxwold, a Domesday Book village where Laurence Sterne was rector. Here he wrote most of *Tristram Shandy* in a house now open as a Sterne museum. Nearby is Ampleforth Abbey, a famous Benedictine school, where we attended mass and heard the schoolboy choir. The Cistercian ruins of Byland and Rievaulx abbeys and Newburgh Priory, where Oliver Cromwell's remains are hidden, are all within a few miles.

This snug retreat should be on every inn lover's list.

Proprietors: Dick and Tricia Goodall. *Facilities:* Bar lounge. *Rooms:* 4 sharing baths. Inexpensive. *Restaurant service:* Luncheon, snacks, dinner. Closed Mondays. *How to get there:* Coxwold is east of Route A19 at the very southern tip of the North Yorkshire moors, southwest of Helmsley. *Telephone:* (034 76) 214.

MANOR FARM

Crackington Haven, Cornwall

> So bright and lovely is the dear old place,
> It seems as though the country's very heart
> Were centered here, and that its antique grace
> Must ever hold it from the world apart,
> Immured it lies among the meadows deep,
> Its flowery stillness beautiful and calm as softest
> sleep.   *John Russell Hayes*

It's hard to realize that this small Cornish manor was on the Domesday List, recorded in 1086. It was owned then by the half brother of William the Conqueror. Today, fine antiques, comfortable seating, lovely colors, fresh flowers, and log fires in winter combine to create an atmosphere of warmth and refinement. We admired handmade bargello covering some window-seat cushions.

Think of the nameless generations who have lived in this farmhouse and tilled these acres. In the rooms where you'll sleep, people in different dress were sleeping a hundred, two hundred, three hundred years ago. Could they have imagined such comforts as electric blankets and shiny modern bathrooms, one for each bedroom? Medieval times are suggested by the stone walls of the dining room. Guests sit together at one table to savor home cooking beautifully served. The reader who suggested we visit Manor Farm wrote, "My wife, a sometimes food critic, thought the cooking the best we had in twenty-one days in England."

A mile from the beach, Manor Farm is surrounded by gardens—camellias bloom in February—and 40 acres of mixed farming. The word fantastic is overused, but it truly applies to the price charged by the Knights.

Proprietors: Muriel and Paul Knight. *Recreational facilities:* Ocean swimming, surfing, sea-fishing, tennis, and riding nearby. *Other facilities:* Living room, games room, laundry, garden. *Rooms:* 4 with bath. Not suitable for children. Very inexpensive. Guests are asked not to smoke in the house. *How to get there:* At the junction of Route A39 and Wainhouse Corner, take a third road marked Crackington Haven and continue to the sea. Stay on the same road as it turns inland again. About a mile up the hill is a telephone booth on the right; turn left a few yards before it, then take the first right and find Manor Farm on the left, about 2 miles from Route A39. *Telephone:* (08403) 304.

Cranbrook, Kent

KENNEL HOLT

> English country life seemed to me the most advanta-
> geous thing in the world.
>
> *Henry James,* 1877

For pure country-house atmosphere, you'll go a long way to find any-
thing to equal Kennel Holt. Its lounge is a spacious beamed and paneled
library that invites evenings of conversation beside a fire. The handhewn beams of the house were put in place in 1588. Under them are
wall-to-wall carpets, comfortable couches, books, and antiques. Every
window has a different view of glorious gardens. Tea is served on the
lawn.

The house is set among England's greatest concentration of gardens
and stately homes open to view. Just two and a half miles away is Sis-
singhurst, perhaps the most beautiful garden in England.

Proprietors: Mr. and Mrs. David Misseldine. *Closed:* Christmas.
Facilities: Lounge, sitting room, garden. *Rooms:* 8 with bath, telephone, and TV. No children under 6. Moderate to expensive. *Credit
cards:* All. *How to get there:* The hotel is signposted on Route A262,
2 miles northwest of Cranbrook. Do not go into the village. *Telephone:*
(0580) 712032.

WILD BOAR HOTEL

> One bright unruffled evening must, if possible, be set
> apart for the splendour, the stillness, the solemnity of
> a three hours' voyage on the lake.
> *William Wordsworth,* 1835

The Wild Boar is a country hotel but not a "country-house" hotel. The atmosphere is that of a professional hotel but one that is full of warmth and hospitality. Part of the building dates back to 1600, and there is a legend that the last boar of Westmorland was killed there.

Traditional red carpeting and red lampshades set off the white plaster walls and low black beams. Open fires in stone fireplaces welcome guests to cozy groupings of cretonne-covered chairs around black oak tables and tavern stools. Here and there are old high-backed settles and Flemish caned chairs. Bedrooms in the newest wing are attractively decorated in modern style, and some have balconies that offer splendid views of the moors and mountains of Cumbria. All come with fruit, flowers, and bottle of sherry.

The restaurant presents a large choice of excellent food and a fine selection of wines. Lake Windermere, one of England's premier resort areas, offers swimming and boating just a few miles away. This hotel will satisfy a fussy traveler.

Manager: Douglas Dale. *Recreational facilities:* Lake swimming, water skiing, scuba-diving school, golf, riding, hunting, trout fishing, and rough shooting nearby. *Facilities for children:* Baby-sitting and -listening. *Other facilities:* Lounge, cocktail bar, garden. *Rooms:* 37 with bath, TV, telephone, tea-making; 1 suite. Ground floor rooms. Off-season rates; breaks; 3- or 4-day Christmas and New Year programs. children under 16 free if sharing. Moderate. *Restaurant service* (no smoking): Luncheon, early and late snacks, tea, supper, dinner. *Credit cards:* Amex, Diners, Master, Visa. *How to get there:* Take exit 36 off superhighway M6. Follow the sign at the end of Kendal bypass marked "Hawkshead via ferry." The hotel is on the right 4 miles along on Route B5284. *Telephone:* (09662) 5225.　　　　[T]

CROSBY LODGE

> The first near glance at this delighted us, for it was manifest that we had come upon a magnificent specimen of architecture of the bygone days when men built for themselves grand habitations—the lordly few of the land, that is.
>
> *James Hissey,* 1889

A relaxed country-house atmosphere prevails at this crenallated, towered, and turreted mock castle secluded in the quiet of the Border country. Ivy covers its walls, and cattle graze in its fields. There are open fires surrounded with leather-topped fire fenders, Victorian tufted sofas, and rose-patterned chintz. Room 6 features an Edwardian suite. Other bedrooms are in traditional style, two with tester beds, but a few have simple modern furniture. Two bedrooms in a converted stable overlook a walled garden.

Before dinner you'll enjoy drinks in a commodious bar with antique Chesterfield furniture. Michael Sedgwick is his own chef, which insures that the food is consistantly delicious. Starters might be duck pâté with orange salad, Stilton croquettes, or avocado mousse with prawns. A loin of veal with Calvados and mushroom sauce was on one menu, as was roast duckling with orange sauce. A choice from a cheese board or desserts from a trolley are followed by petits fours and coffee.

A dip into Scotland would be a fine day's outing for those who haven't time to tour that land of bagpipes and heather.

Proprietors: Michael and Patricia Sedgwick. *Closed:* December 24–late January. *Facilities:* Lounge, cocktail bar, garden. *Rooms:* 11 with bath, telephone, and TV. Weekend breaks off season; discount for children under 12. Moderate to expensive. *Restaurant service:* Luncheon, snacks, dinner. *Credit cards:* Amex, Diners, Visa. *How to get there:* The hotel is on B6264, 4 miles east of Carlisle. From M6, take exit 44 and follow the signs for Brampton. *Telephone:* (0228 73) 618.

THE DEDHAM VALE HOTEL

A comfortable house is a great source of happiness.
Sydney Smith, 1843

The Dedham Vale is not only comfortable, it is beautiful. This country-house hotel was acquired a few years ago by the owner of the luxurious Maison Talbooth and the well-known Le Talbooth restaurant. Located between the two of them, it stands on terraced lawns amidst gardens of cultivated beauty. Bedrooms are decorated with sophistication to the same glamourous standard as those of Maison Talbooth, but they are a bit smaller and less expensive.

The Terrace Restaurant, of Edwardian-style glass reminiscent of the 1851 Crystal Palace, was added to the original Regency building. Its sunny colors, greenery, and flowers echo the gardens outside its windows. Featured is an elaborate black and brass French rotisserie in a green-tiled alcove on which steaks, kebabs, game, legs of lamb, and home-grown chickens are grilled. Among items on the menu are vegetarian specialities and desserts served from trolleys. For a change, guests can walk to the riverside Le Talbooth for meals.

Proprietor: Gerald Milsom. *Recreational facilities:* Riding, golf, tennis, and squash nearby. *Other facilities:* Lounge, cocktail bar, garden. *Rooms:* 6 with bath, telephone, and TV. Moderate to expensive. *Restaurant service:* Luncheon (except Saturday), dinner. *Credit cards:* Amex, Diners, Master, Visa. *How to get there:* Dedham is 7 miles north of Colchester, off Route A12. The hotel is on Stratford Road, 1 mile south of the village center, where you should ask directions. *Telephone:* (0206) 322273. [T]

MAISON TALBOOTH

These scenes made me a painter.

John Constable

The Vale of Dedham is known throughout the world from the paintings of Constable, who immortalized the views you will see from your windows. Maison Talbooth has been decorated by a top London designer, who combined many antiques with modern touches such as a little bar in each bedroom, where peanuts and ice are placed at six each evening. It has been said that for each of the glamorous bathrooms there is a glamorous bedroom. Some tubs are round and others sunken. Despite all the luxury, this is a warm and friendly hotel, where guests meet as at a private house party.

A Continental breakfast is served, and a light sandwich lunch may be had in the charming living room or in the garden beyond the French doors. For other meals guests go to Le Talbooth, a celebrated restaurant half a mile away, or to the Dedham Vale Hotel, just down the road. Gerald Milsom developed his country-house hotel, Maison Talbooth, after his restaurant, Le Talbooth, was already famous. Its ancient half-timber work of closely set studs filled with wattle and daub was painted by Constable. That painting hangs in the National Gallery of Scotland, in Edinburgh, but a copy is on the wall of the restaurant's entrance hall. The name Le Talbooth derives from the time when tolls were collected at a bridge crossing the River Stour, which flows beside the gardens where you may sit and sip a before-dinner drink. The restaurant has a fine wine list.

Proprietor: Gerald Milsom. *Recreational facilities:* Riding, golf, tennis, and squash a short drive away. *Other facilities:* Drawing room, garden. *Rooms:* 10 with bath, TV, and telephone. Suitable for wheelchair guests. Expensive to very expensive. *Restaurant service:* Luncheon, dinner (at Le Talbooth). *Credit cards:* Amex, Diners, Master, Visa. *How to get there:* Dedham is 7 miles north of Colchester, off Route A12. The hotel is on Stratford Road, 1 mile south of the village center, where you should ask directions. *Telephone:* (0206) 322367. *Agent in the United States:* Abercrombie and Kent.   [T]

Diddlebury, Shropshire

GLEBE FARM

Sheltered, when the rain blew over the hill it was,
Sunny all day when the days of summer were long,
Beyond all rumour of laboring towns it was,
But at dawn and evening its trees were noisy with song.
J.C. Squire, 1914

To be at Glebe Farm is to be in the sixteenth century, nicely modernized for today's travelers. Michael Wilkes farmed 123 acres here for
many years, raising cattle, sheep, and poultry. In order to stay in their
Tudor home when he retired, the Wilkes turned it into a guest house.

One room has become a small cocktail bar where Michael presides
before dinner. He is a lively host who likes to mingle with his guests,
encouraging a congenial atmosphere. After dinner he joined us in the

living room, telling us about life in this prosperous farming country. The room's plaster walls, with black beams embedded, were built by an old method called wattle and daub. Velvet draperies, a grand piano, a slant-top desk, various antiques, and shelves of books about gardening and silver convey an air of refinement and good taste.

The kitchen is the baliwick of Mrs. Wilkes, and her fine cooking is in keeping with the house. Beef, lamb, duck, and poultry are all produced on the home farm, which has been taken over by a son. So are milk, cream, butter, eggs, and vegetables. Make a dinner reservation when you book a room. The Wilkes take a few nonresidents for dinner when they have space. If you arrive unexpected late in the afternoon, they might have a bedroom for you but not a table for dinner. Everyone sits at separate tables at one time in a flagstoned, heavily beamed dining room that dates from 1580. The view from its windows is across the garden to a Saxon church with a fortified tower for which Glebe Farm was once the rectory. The Wilkes built an annex next to the house to provide four more bedrooms. We prefer to stay with the old, delighting in floors that slant and doorways through which we must duck.

A short walk from the house takes you to the foot of Wenlock Edge, made famous by A.E. Houseman's poem "A Shropshire Lad." This beautiful part of England near the Welsh border does not attract large numbers of tourists. In high season it would be a more enjoyable region to tour than the thronged roads of the southwest or the lake district.

Proprietors: Eileen and Michael Wilkes. *Closed:* Early November through February. *Recreational facilities:* Riding nearby. *Other facilities:* Living room, cocktail bar, garden. *Rooms:* 8, 2 with bath, all with tea-making. No children under 10. Inexpensive. *Restaurant service:* Dinner by reservation. *How to get there:* From Route A49 between Shrewsbury and Ludlow, take Route B4368 5 miles to Diddlebury. At the telephone booth, turn right to Glebe Farm. *Telephone:* (058476) 221.

Dorchester-on-Thames, Oxfordshire

THE GEORGE

> Those towns that we call thorowfaires have sumptuous
> innes builded for the receiving of such travellers and
> strangers as passe to and fro . . . Everie man may have
> for his monie how great or how little varietie of vit-
> tels himself shall think expedient . . . if his chamber
> be once appointed he may carrie the kei with him so
> long as he lodgeth there.
>
> *William Harrison,* 1563

The George was one of the "sumptuous innes" receiving strangers in
1563. It is believed to have been built to accommodate visitors to a

twelfth-century Augustinian priory. Its overhanging gables, whitewashed walls, and mellow brickwork, its exposed beams and open log fires, are as warm and inviting today as they were to the long-ago travelers.

In the high-raftered dining hall, thought to be the original monks' brewhouse and one of the best examples of medieval domestic architecture left in England, you'll dine on food fresh from local farms and the hotel's garden. Some memorable wines are stored deep in the old cellars, and a selection of real ale is to be found in the tavern.

We first stopped here for lunch quite a few years ago and were charmed with the building. Now, different owners have since renovated The George, and it boasts twentieth-century comforts. For an appointment with the past, stay for a night and ask for a room with a four-poster bed.

Manager: Michael Thompson. *Recreational facilities:* Boat hire and trips nearby. *Other facilities:* TV lounge, public bar, garden. *Rooms:* 17 with bath, all with telephone, TV, and tea-making. Ground-floor rooms, 2- or 3-day weekend reduction. Moderate to expensive. *Restaurant:* Luncheon, snacks, dinner. *How to get there:* The inn is on Route A423 in the village. Guests can be met at Heathrow airport or at the train in Didcot or Oxford. *Telephone:* (0865) 340404. [T]

East Grinstead, West Sussex

GRAVETYE MANOR

> Of all the things that the English have invented . . .
> the most perfect, the most characteristic, the only one
> they have mastered . . . so that it becomes a compen-
> dious illustration of their social genius and their man-
> ners, is the well-appointed, well-ministered, well-filled
> country house.
>
> *Henry James,* 1905

Both within and without, this place is beautiful. Wood fires burn fra-
grantly; guests meet in the paneled bar; the staff is solicitous and friendly; the wine cellar is one of the best in England; such dishes as hare and

venison appear on the menu, along with Continental and English cuisine. Gravetye Manor is one of the most luxurious country-house hotels in Britain, distinguished but not stuffy.

The manor was built in 1598. Its most notable owner was William Robinson, one of the greatest gardeners of all time and author of *The English Flower Garden*. He bought the manor, and the 1,000 acres in which it stands, in 1884. Here he realized his idea of creating an English natural garden, now admired and copied all over the world. He paneled many of the rooms with oak from his woods, and today each bedroom is named for a different tree he planted—Ash, Birch, Beech, Holly.

In an earlier century the manor was used as a smugglers' hideout where plunder was distributed. Part of Smuggler's Lane still trails through the estate, which is a bird sanctuary. Gravetye Manor captures the spirit of English country-house hospitality. It is just a short drive from Gatwick airport and is one of the few English members of the Relais et Chateaux Hotels, an association of renowned privately owned country hotels.

Proprietor: Peter Herbert. *Recreational facilities:* Tennis, squash, and riding a short drive away. *Rooms:* 14 with bath, TV, and telephone. Advance reservation essential; 2-day minimum on weekends. No children under 7. Expensive to very expensive. *Restaurant service:* Luncheon, dinner. *How to get there:* Signs for Gravetye Manor are on Route B2110 west of East Grinstead village and on B2028 coming from Brighton. The hotel will arrange for guests to be met at Gatwick or Heathrow Airports and put guests on a train for London at Three Bridges Station a day or two later. *Telephone:* (0342) 810567. *Agent in the United States:* David Mitchell.   [T]

SUMMER LODGE

> She dipped down a hill . . . into the small town or village
> of Evershead . . . she made a halt there and break-
> fasted a second time . . . at a cottage by the church.
> *Thomas Hardy,* 1891

The thatched cottage where Tess had her breakfast is still by the church
in Evershot, the Evershead of Thomas Hardy's *Tess of the D'Uber-
villes.* Just down the road is the fine country-house hotel called Summer Lodge. Locally it is said that the illustrious author, who was a
qualified architect, drew the plans for one wing of the hotel.

Nigel and Margaret Corbett escaped London to create this country
house with a relaxed and informal atmosphere. Care, comfort, and
courtesy are the keynotes. Nigel, who was working in the garden,
greeted us cheerfully and took our bags as we walked from the parking area. We were soon enjoying afternoon tea with homemade shortbread before a fire.

The lounge is a gracious room, light and sunny, with plump chairs
on which to read in comfort the magazines and books about Dorset
that are on hand on antique tables. Bedrooms are pretty and comfortable, with views over gardens and fields.

The Corbetts' five-course dinner is commended in food guides. If
you cannot eat certain things, or wish a vegetarian dinner, discuss the
menu of the day with them. The wine list is above-average.

Summer Lodge is a hospitable place of quiet character that guests
return to again and again.

Proprietors: Margaret and Nigel Corbett. *Recreational facilities:*
Tennis and outdoor pool at the house; riding and golf nearby. *Other
facilities:* Drawing room, TV room, cocktail bar, garden. *Rooms:* 17
with bath, telephone, and tea-making. 2-day reduction; off-season
rates. No childen under 8. Expensive. *Restaurant service:* Dinner by
reservation. *Credit cards:* Master, Visa. *How to get there:* Evershot is
west off Route A37 at the village of Batcombe, between Dorchester
and Yeovil. *Telephone:* (0935) 83424.

THE COURT

> My heart is warm with the friends I make,
> And better friends I'll not be knowing . . .
> *Edna St. Vincent Millay*

At this delightful home you'll really feel as if you are visiting friends. A reader suggested we see it, saying it was her favorite stop of a six-week trip, even though she stayed in some well-known luxurious country-house hotels. She became friends with the proprietors and planned to return and stay with them again.

The house is unique in that it dates back only to 1933 but was constructed of materials from an old mansion that was pulled down on the property. A splendid oak staircase was saved intact. We enjoyed sitting before a fire in a large, comfortable living room furnished with antiques. The sunny dining room, with blue and white plates displayed in a cabinet, looks onto a heather garden. Ask to see the secret door hidden in a bookcase.

Bedrooms are large, and although none have private baths there are plenty of bathrooms, some with showers, which are by no means common in English houses. Two of the five bedrooms are singles (at no supplementary charge). Dinner is a set meal, but changes can be made if the menu offers something you do not like. Guests are welcome to bring their own drinks, as The Court has no license. Fruits, vegetables, and milk from a Jersey herd are right from the 60 acres, which include river and woodland walks, a rock garden, and a pond with ducks and geese. This is an informal place where people talk to each other. It gives wonderful value for your money.

Proprietors: Peggy Lazenby and Maureen Stephens. *Closed:* Mid-October to Easter. *Recreational facilities:* Golf nearby. *Other facilities:* Living room, garden. *Rooms:* 5 sharing baths, with tea-making. 2-night minimum stay. Not suitable for children. Very inexpensive. *How to get there:* From Route A356 in Frampton, northwest of Dorchester, take Southover Street across the River Frome. Then take the first left and find The Court on your left. *Telephone:* (0300) 20242.

WOODLANDS

Tired with the town and all its noisy sway,
With eager haste I make the northern way,
Leave pomp and vanity, fatigue and care,
For sweet tranquility with rural fare.
Thomas Maude, 1771

Woodlands is a warm guest house with an air of friendly comfort. The Georgian house, once the center of an estate, is sited to take advantage of views across the Ribble valley, where sheep graze on grassy fields crisscrossed by stone walls. Here and there is a little stone farmhouse and byre tucked into a fold in the dales.

Welcoming bedrooms are named for birds of Yorkshire—Curlew, Heron, Chaffinch, Wren. All beds have continental quilts, and there is no supplement for a single room. The food, always fresh and with generous helpings, is especially good here: Roger Callan is a professional who lectures at a catering school. Thoughtful extras include early morning tea brought to your room with a newspaper. Margaret Callan brings late evening tea and coffee to the lounge, an attractive room with green velvet upholstery.

The village of Giggleswick is mentioned in the Domesday Book. In bustling Settle across the river, the open market is held every Tuesday. This highly recommended guest house is a good center for exploring both the Yorkshire dales and the Cumbrian lakes.

Proprietors: Margaret and Roger Callan. *Closed:* Christmas and New Year's Day. *Recreational facilities:* Indoor pool and squash a short walk away; tennis a short drive away. *Other facilities:* Living room, TV lounge, garden. *Rooms:* 9, 3 with bath; TV available. Ground-floor rooms. Winter breaks; reduction for children sharing. No children under 12. Inexpensive. *How to get there:* Woodlands is at the end of a cul-de-sac, signposted "The Mains" on Route A65, opposite the sign for Giggleswick. *Telephone:* (072 92) 2576.

COMBE HOUSE

I dislike feeling at home when I'm abroad.
George Bernard Shaw

You won't feel at home in Combe House—not unless home is just slightly less opulent than Blenheim Palace. Magnificent is the word for this Elizabethan mansion set in a beautiful estate. Grand as it is, however, it isn't intimidating. There's a "house-party" feeling to the place. Guests, staff, and owners mingle cordially.

Antique lovers will enjoy the fine architecture—ornate plasterwork ceilings, rococo fireplaces, rich paneling set off by vivacious colors as well as the furniture and paintings, many of them brought from the ancestral Boswell home, Auchinleck House, in Scotland. John Boswell is a direct descendant of *the* Boswell, of Boswell and Johnson fame.

In the Great Hall, guests sink into deep couches and chairs covered in lovely English floral fabrics, mostly grouped around a roaring fire. Enjoying a traditional Devon cream tea here, after a brisk walk to view the rhododendron, magnolia, and solid old trees on the extensive grounds, made us wonder if we hadn't stepped back into a Victorian novel. Bedrooms are spacious, with comfortable upholstered chairs.

Therese Boswell is French. She attended the Cordon Bleu school and runs the kitchen with the help of a team of Cordon Bleu cooks. The cuisine is French in inspiration, using the best of local fish, meat, and vegetables, some right from the estate gardens.

Gittisham is a showpiece village of pale stone houses, thatched cottages, and a tiny towered church, all of which now belong to the National Trust.

Proprietors: John and Therese Boswell. *Closed:* Mid-January–mid-February. *Recreational facilities:* Riding on the estate; ocean swimming, tennis, squash, golf, boat rental, boat trips, sea-fishing, and hunting nearby. *Facilities for children:* Baby-sitting (if arranged in time), children's supper. *Other facilities:* Hall lounge, drawing room, cocktail lounge, limited laundry service, garden. *Rooms:* 11 with bath, telephone, and TV; 1 suite. Winter breaks; 4-day Christmas program. Moderate to expensive. *Credit cards:* Amex, Diners, Master, Visa. *How to get there:* The house is signposted just south of Honiton on Route A30, the main London-to-Exeter road. *Telephone:* (0404) 2756. *Agent in the United States:* Abercrombie and Kent.

Goudhurst, Kent

STAR AND EAGLE

> We were disposed to sleep under the very oldest
> English architecture . . . we would be shown by
> delightfully narrow, crooked, and every way possi-
> ble inconvenient stairways . . . into long, steep-roofed
> rooms.
>
> *Frederick Law Olmsted,* 1850

The Tabard Inn, from which Chaucer's pilgrims began their journey
into Kent, vanished long ago, but the Star and Eagle was its contemporary; those pilgrims might have stopped here. The narrow, crooked
stairways are in every way inconvenient, especially when one is carry-
ing luggage. The roughhewn beams and low-linteled doorways were
put in place by medieval craftsmen six hundred years ago, when peo-

ple were much shorter than they are today. Anyone over 5 feet tall must take great care, as he wends his way to bed through tortuous passages, that he doesn't give his head a jolly good crump, as they say in England. To experience such antiquity makes any necessary contortions worthwhile.

Bedrooms are bright and comfortable, fully carpeted, and with new furniture except for one bedroom with a four-poster. Fine bathrooms, some with oak beams embedded in walls, are new too. Everything is fresh—the antiquity does not include mustiness. The restaurant is reasonable and very busy, with many patrons from the area. Medallions of beef in chianti or Scotch salmon are among offerings that include traditional grills and roasts. Start with farmhouse vegetable soup; end with a homemade dessert from the selection on a sideboard.

In the bar is an inglenook fireplace with a nook to warm a tankard of beer. The village has seen little change in four hundred years. The inn was headquarters for the Hawkhurst Gang, eighteenth-century desperadoes. These smugglers and robbers terrorized the district until the village formed a militia to resist them. A pitched battle was fought, and the gang leader was shot in what is now the inn's parking lot. Tunnels led to both the historic Saint Mary's church next to the inn and the local manor house, Pattendene, which tells something of who protected the smugglers.

This aged inn in this ancient village is no archaic museum piece. Travelers in centuries past, in different dress, with different customs, have sat before its fires from feudal times to the present. History lives on at the Star and Eagle.

Manager: Michel and Karin Dimet. *Recreational facilities:* Riding nearby. *Facilities:* Lounge, bar, garden. *Rooms:* 11, 9 with bath, all with TV, telephone, and tea-making. Breaks; reduction for children under 12 sharing (under 2 free). Moderate. *Restaurant service:* Luncheon, early and late snacks, dinner. *Credit cards:* Amex, Master, Visa. *How to get there:* Goudhurst is on Route A262, a few miles east of Royal Tunbridge Wells. *Telephone:* (0580) 211512.

Grasmere, Cumbria

MICHAELS NOOK

> Upon the forest-side at Grasmere Vale
> There dwelt a Shepherd, Michael was his name.
> *William Wordsworth*

The name of this hotel salutes the memory of the shepherd Michael, whose cottage-dwelling was on this very site. A collector of fine antiques, Reginald Gifford runs Michaels Nook in a manner that conveys the atmosphere of an elegant home. There is no reception desk. Immediate impressions are of fireglow, gleaming silver, and rich old mahogany. Porcelain foot baths, old copper pans, and other such objects are imaginatively used as cachepots for fresh flowers and plants. A beautiful staircase sweeps upstairs, where some of the furniture was designed at the same time as the house to match the bedroom chimneypieces. In the dining room the china is Coalport, the crystal is Stuart, the silver is sterling, and the prices are high. The food, consistently praised by leading restaurant guides, was written up in *Gourmet* magazine. All guests book for dinner, bed, and breakfast.

Tables show off collections under glass, and Victorian domes protect gilt clocks. Anyone who likes to browse through antique shops will adore this place. Mr. Gifford has another hotel, the Wordsworth, in the center of Grasmere village. Renovation of the old place took eighteen months. Delicate plasterwork was restored, and many antiques are among the furnishings. With thirty-six bedrooms, an indoor heated pool, a sauna, and a solarium, it is more impersonal than Michaels Nook. The price is about the same, and most credit cards are accepted.

Proprietor: Reginald Gifford. *Recreational facilities:* Lake swimming, indoor pool, and sauna a short drive away. *Rooms:* 9 with bath, TV, and telephone; 2 suites. 3-day minimum stay on weekends in season. 4-day Christmas program. Very expensive. *Restaurant service:* Luncheon and dinner (by reservation). *How to get there:* Find the Swan hotel on Route A591. Turn uphill beside it and drive right into Michaels Nook. Avoid the Grasmere village center. *Telephone:* (09665) 496. *Agent in the United States:* Abercrombie and Kent.   [T]

SWAN HOTEL

Who does not know the famous Swan?
William Wordsworth, 1819

A roadside inn immortalized by Wordsworth in his poem "The Waggoner," this old hostelry, which was established about three hundred years ago, has retained its hospitable character over the centuries.

The beamed lounge, with a chair that belonged to the great poet himself and warmed with old oaken furniture displaying antique china, says, "Welcome," as does the informal garden. The bedrooms are mostly modern.

In 1854 Hawthorne wrote, "I . . . passed the Swan inn, where Scott used to go daily and get a draught of liquor, when he was visiting

Wordsworth, who had no wine or other inspiriting fluid in his house.''

Manager: Peter Coward. *Recreational facilities:* Lake swimming, sauna; and indoor pool nearby. *Other facilities:* Lounge, TV lounge, public bar, garden. *Rooms:* 41, 25 with bath. Reduction for children under 14 sharing (under 5 free); winter breaks; Christmas program. Moderate to expensive. *Restaurant service:* Luncheon, snacks, tea, dinner. *Credit cards:* Amex, Carte Blanche, Diners, Master, Visa. *How to get there:* The hotel is on Route A591 in Grasmere. *Telephone:* (09665) 551. *Agent in the United States:* THF.   [T]

WHITE MOSS HOUSE

> There was a quiet splendor, almost grandeur, about Grasmere vale . . . a kind of monumental beauty and dignity that agreed well with one's conception of the loftier strain of its poet.
>
> *John Burroughs,* 1884

White Moss House has beauty and dignity too, though it is not monumental. The house belonged to Wordsworth, although the poet never lived in it, and today it is an unusual hotel whose perfection of detail in both food and service has earned it renown.

There are only five bedrooms in the main house. Each offers books, magazines, a map of the Lake District, shoe cleaners, notepaper, a sewing kit, a hair dryer, and fresh flowers, and each is furnished with an assortment of antiques mixed with necessary newer things. The Dixons have an extensive knowledge of the area and a great love for it. They will advise you on how best to spend a short or long stay, and particularly recommend some fell walking, a very popular British pastime.

Peter Dixon is in charge of all the cooking, which *Gourmet* magazine called outstanding. Everyone sits down to dinner at 8:00, and there is no choice of main course. Leg of Lakeland lamb, roast Coniston duckling, and poached Solway salmon are some of the entrées offered on different nights. There is a choice of three or four desserts that might include apricot brandy flan, raspberry shortcake, homemade raisin and rum ice cream, Westmorland raisin and nut pie with rum cream. English cheeses with White Moss oat biscuits, then coffee and mints, follow the desserts. All bookings are for dinner, as well as bed and breakfast.

In addition to the rooms in the main house, there is Brockstone cottage, a short drive or an "energetic" walk away, with living room and two bedrooms. This pleasant hotel, with a tradition of personal service, is for quiet people who will enjoy talking with the other guests in a homelike atmosphere.

Proprietors: Sue and Peter Dixon. *Closed:* November to mid-March. *Recreational facilities:* Tennis, squash, riding, lake and river swimming, and an indoor pool a short drive away. *Other facilities:* Lounge, garden. *Rooms:* 7 with bath and TV. 3-day reduction. Not suitable for children. Expensive. *Restaurant service:* Dinner by reservation. *How to get there:* The hotel is on Route A591 between Ambleside and Grasmere. *Telephone:* (096 65) 295.

Greta Bridge, North Yorkshire

MORRITT ARMS

To our great joy we discovered a comfortable room,
with drawn curtains, and a most blazing fire. In half
an hour they gave us a smoking supper, and a bottle
of mulled port.

Charles Dickens

The great author wrote the words above to his wife from Greta Bridge
while he was at the George Inn, long gone. The Morritt Arms is dedicated to the memory of Dickens and the George, and a right good job
has been made of it. The atmosphere of the dark-paneled public rooms,
with Jacobean furniture, firelight bouncing off a gleam of polished copper, "ceilings heavy with massive beams," makes us think that
Dickens's own words were rightly used as a guide for the interior design:

"a delicious perspective of warmth and brightness—when the ruddy gleam of the fire streaming through the old red curtains of the common room, seemed to bring with it, as part of itself, a pleasant hum of voices, and a fragrant odour of steaming grog and rare tobacco, all steeped, as it were, in the cheerful glow."

From here you can explore the haunting beauty of the lonely Yorkshire moors and dales. Sir Walter Scott called this countryside "one of the most enviable places I have ever seen." It is the setting for his famous *Rokeby*, dedicated to his friend John Morritt with the words "the scene of which is laid in his beautiful demesne of Rokeby." Stop for a bar lunch or tea if you don't stay overnight.

Proprietors: David and John Mulley. *Recreational facilities:* Tennis and riding a short drive away. *Facilities for children:* Playground. *Other facilities:* Lounge, public bar, garden. *Rooms:* 28, 16 with bath, all with TV. Reduction; 2-day breaks; reduction for children sharing. Inexpensive to moderate. *Restaurant service:* Snacks all day, tea, dinner. *Credit cards:* Amex, Diners, Master, Visa. *How to get there:* Greta Bridge is about 3 miles south of Barnard Castle on Route A66. *Telephone:* (0833) 27232.

[T]

Grimsthorpe, Lincolnshire

BLACK HORSE INN

> The English wayside inn is a feature of the English countryside . . . at its best there is a cosiness and cheer about it which warm the heart, as its quaintness and savour of past days keep alive the sense of romantic travel.
>
> *Richard Le Gallienne,* 1915

The Black Horse Inn is a hostelry of individuality from its furnishings to its food, but its food is what it is famous for. Lauded in all restaurant guides, it specializes in the very best English cooking: a family member helps guests choose from the large menu; vegetables come from a garden across the road, freshly picked and cooked to order; herbs are from the inn's own herb garden: other items are from nearby farms. A memorable dinner might feature Elizabethan pork, deviled lamb kidneys with brandy, or Mrs. Beeton's beafsteak, kidney, and mushroom pie. For luncheon you could try shepherd's pie or chicken livers Osbert Sitwell. Some desserts are from old recipes, some are original: honey meringues, treacle tart, or apple pie with cream. The sophisticated and charming Fishers, who own the Black Horse, have demonstrated their cooking on various TV stations during an American tour and have been featured on the BBC.

Your first welcome will be the warmth of a log fire. The decorating does justice to the food—stone walls, different kinds of antique tables, Adam firedogs, silver candelabra, chrysanthemums, gourds and pine cones arranged about stuffed pheasants. The bar has walls of natural plaster, black beams, and a red rug. There's old oak, a coal fire glowing on a stone hearth, a friendly black dog.

Bedrooms are small but comfortable, pretty with floral chintz and fresh flowers. There is a nice single room with bath at the same rate per person as the doubles.

This Black Horse Inn is unpretentious but first class, with meticulous attention to detail. The duke and duchess of Gloucester have been guests. The family will help plan your day trips, recommending the best places to shop. You can drive to nearby Peterborough and take a train into London for the day.

Proprietors: Kay and Joyce Fisher. *Closed:* Sundays and Christmas. *Recreational facilities:* Outdoor pool, tennis, riding, and sailing nearby. *Other facilities:* TV lounge, cocktail bar, garden. *Rooms:* 4 with bath and tea-making. 2-day minimum advance reservation. Moderate. *Restaurant service:* Luncheon, snacks, dinner. *Credit cards:* Amex, Master, Visa. *How to get there:* Grimsthorpe is on Route A151 between Bourne and Grantham. *Telephone:* (077 832) 247.

Hawkhurst, Kent

TUDOR ARMS

The County of Kent is rich in medows pastures and pleasant Groves, and wonderfully aboundeth with Apples and Cheeries.

Celia Fiennes, 1697

At this unpretentious, sunny inn in the weald of Kent, renowned as the garden of England, you will find a courteous welcome. The feature of the hotel is its exceptional garden, where drinks and snacks are served under the trees when weather permits.

Pretty floral draperies, plants, fresh flowers, books, magazines, a nice old desk, and a copper chestnut roaster give the lounge a pleasant, bright aspect, although the furniture is plain. In the bar, the glow of a fire sets off nice old paneling, and a cabinet holds small gifts for sale. The dining room features some French and Italian dishes and uses fresh local produce; bedrooms are comfortably modern, bathrooms are almost new, and the whole place shines.

Some cities within easy reach are busy, crowded Canterbury, Eastbourne, the Cinque Ports of Sussex and Kent, and the port of Dover.

Manager: David Hill. *Recreational facilities:* Tennis at the hotel; riding and sauna nearby. *Facilities for children:* Baby-sitting; playground. *Other facilities:* Lounge, cocktail bar, public bar, garden. *Rooms:* 14, 11 with bath; all with TV and tea-making. Reductions, reduction for children sharing; Christmas program. Moderate. *Restaurant service:* Luncheon, early and late snacks, tea, dinner. *Credit cards:* Amex, Diners, Master, Visa. *How to get there:* The hotel is on Route A268, 1 mile from Hawkhurst on the road to Rye. *Telephone:* (058 05) 2312. *Agent in the United States:* Best Western.   [T]

Helford, Cornwall

RIVERSIDE

> When the east wind blows up Helford River the shining waters become troubled and disturbed, and the little waves beat angrily upon the sandy shores.
> *Daphne duMaurier,* 1941

Helford is a picturebook Cornish village evocative of the stories of Daphne duMaurier. Reached by winding country lanes, its houses are set haphazardly on steep narrow streets that climb both banks of a tidal creek off the Helford River. This is hardly a place you'd expect to find one of England's top restaurants, but that is what *The Good Food Guide* called Riverside when it named it the "best restaurant with rooms" in England.

Converted from several white cottages, Riverside has pretty bedrooms of various sizes, some with slanted ceilings and some with outside entrances reached by flagstone steps. A small attractive lounge has cane furniture. Here and there between the buildings are little garden terraces with outdoor furniture, where guests can breakfast on warm croissants and homemade marmalade while watching boats below. Owners and staff are friendly and welcoming.

Dinner is an expensive fixed-price meal, with about eight choices for each course. Riverside's new owner intends to continue the hotel's reputation, under its former owners, of having one of the best restaurants in Britain.

Proprietors: Susie Darrell. *Closed:* November to mid-March. *Recreational facilities:* Ocean and river swimming, golf, riding, boat hire, and boat trips nearby. *Other facilities:* Lounge, garden. *Rooms:* 7 with bath and TV. Moderate to expensive. *Restaurant service:* Dinner. *How to get there:* From Helston, take route 3083 until you pass the Air Station. At the mini-roundabout, turn left onto B3293, signposted for Coverack. After passing Garras, take the next left to Newtown. At the "T" junction in Newtown, bear right, then left to Helford. The Riverside car park is opposite the public car park as you enter the village. *Telephone:* (032 623) 443.

HERNES

> An old English family mansion is a fertile subject for
> study. It abounds with illustrations of former times,
> and traces of the tastes, and humors, and manners,
> of successive generations.
>
> *Washington Irving,* 1822

For five generations, Hernes has been home to one English family. Surrounded by lawns, trees, and gardens, and with an outdoor heated swimming pool, the house, begun in the sixteenth century, is part of a 400-acre farm estate.

Gillian Ovey says she loves to entertain; and, to help pay for her children's education, she prefers entertaining paying guests to getting a conventional job. Gillian is warm and friendly. Upon our arrival she brought us afternoon tea and sat down for a chat. We were in a gracious, wood-paneled living room—one of those large entrance rooms so typical of old English houses and called The Hall. Chairs and sofa covered with brocade and velvet were grouped informally before a wide hearth where flames snapped. Brass firetools gleamed. Magazines and brochures of nearby attractions were on handsome old tables, along with fresh flowers in Chinese porcelain vases and bibelots collected by former generations. An ancestor portrait or two hung on the paneling, and a grand piano in one corner held framed family photographs. The room was welcoming.

Our spacious bedroom was the loveliest of our trip. In our bathroom, besides the usual fixtures, were a bidet, two antique mahogany chests of drawers, a cheval mirror, and, best of all, a fire going in a stove set into a former fireplace.

We knocked on the door at four o'clock without a reservation, but don't do the same. Call ahead so you can have dinner with the Oveys and savor home-produced meat and game, vegetables, milk, butter, and eggs from the farm. Gillian serves a four-course dinner, but you can ask for a light supper. Hernes is not licensed, but guests may bring their own drinks. Gillian told us she'd have been happy to fix a meal for us but Richard was holding a church-related meeting in their dining room that evening. When we returned from dinner, we relaxed again before the fire and met some of Richard's guests while we drank coffee Gillian brought in.

Henley-on-Thames is central to Windsor, Eton, Ascot, Wimbledon, Oxford, Bath, and storybook Cotswold villages. As it is only 35 minutes from Heathrow, a stay at Hernes would be a memorable introduction to England.

Proprietors: Gillian and Richard Ovey. *Recreational facilities:* Outdoor pool at the house; riding, boat rental, and boat trips on the Thames nearby. *Other facilities:* Living room, billiards room, garden. *Rooms:* 3 with bath. Not suitable for young children. Moderate. *How to get there:* From the bridge across the Thames River into Henley, go straight for a block and turn left onto Duke Street. Turn right onto Greys Road. Drive along this winding road until you reach the end of the 30 MPH area. Hernes is about 200 yards further along on the right. *Telephone:* (0491) 573245.

Henley-on-Thames, Oxfordshire

RED LION HOTEL

Who'er has travelled life's dull round,
Where'er his stages may have been,
May sigh to think how oft he found
The warmest welcome at an inn.
                    William Shenstone, 1737

"We happened to lie this night at the inn at Henley, where Shenstone wrote these lines," said Boswell. Yes, this is the place where Shenstone is said to have scratched on a window pane what are probably the most familiar words written about inns.

The Red Lion, a storied inn, was given the name of Anglers Inn in Dickens's *Our Mutual Friend.* Charles I and George IV slept under its ancient timbers, and a room was always kept ready for the original Duke of Marlborough, for a break in his trip between London and

Blenheim. Bedrooms are named for the famous historical characters who have visited this most renowned of old coaching inns: Queen Charlotte, Dr. Johnson, Prince Rupert.

Directly across the Thames from the famous rowing club, the Red Lion offers grandstand viewing of the Royal Henley Regatta, since 1839 the principal gathering of amateur oarsmen from all over the world. Ask for a room overlooking the river. We awakened our first morning in England to sunlight dancing on the ceiling, reflected from the famous waters. Crews in rowing shells were already at practice. This was *England*, no doubt about that.

Henley-on-Thames, a bustling town of about 12,000 not far from Heathrow Airport, is a wonderful place to start a tour of Britain. You will be quickly immersed in English life as you go in and out of stores, have afternoon tea in little tearooms, walk beside the Thames watching all the boat traffic, stop in pubs that cater to locals, not tourists. There are fine antique shops for browsing, but prices are high. If you want just a quick look at London, the trains run frequently, as many people commute.

The old red-brick facade of the Red Lion, mantled with wisteria and banked with flowers, has changed little over the centuries. Ashley Sterry wrote of it,

> Tis a finely toned, picturesque, sunshiny, place,
> Recalling a dozen old stories;
> With a rare British, good-natured, ruddy-hued face,
> Suggesting old wines and old Tories.

Recreational facilities: Boat rental and boat trips on the Thames a short walk away. *Other facilities:* Lounge, cocktail bar, public bar. *Rooms:* 27, 20 with bath, all with TV and telephone. Moderate to expensive. *Credit cards:* Amex, Master, Visa. *How to get there:* The Red Lion is on Hart Street. Trains from London are frequent. *Telephone:* (0491) 572161. [T]

Horton-cum-Studley, Oxfordshire

STUDLEY PRIORY

> There are long corridors, an intricate arrangement of
> passages, and an up-and-down meandering of stair-
> cases, amid which it would be no marvel to encounter
> some forgotten guest who had gone astray a hundred
> years ago, and was still seeking for his bedroom while
> the rest of his generation were in their graves.
>
> *Nathaniel Hawthorne,* 1855

If Studley Priory looks familiar, you probably saw the movie *A Man
for All Seasons*, in which it portrays the home of Sir Thomas More.
A twelfth-century Benedictine convent turned into an Elizabethan
manor after the dissolution of the nunneries by Henry VIII, its woods
were ordered cut down by Cardinal Wolsey to build Christ Church at
Oxford. Studley Priory fits Hawthorne's description quoted above, but
it was a private home at the time Hawthorne lived in England.

We went through a network of passages, corridors, and stairs to
reach our room, thinking perhaps we should have unwound a ball of
twine behind us to find our way back. Our bedroom was attractively
furnished, though not with old things, and if you hope to get one appointed with antiques, ask well ahead. You will pay a bit extra for the
one with a magnificent Elizabethan tester bed constructed from linen-
fold paneling. Coats of arms of the Croke family, who owned Studley
Priory for more than three hundred years, line the cornice of the reception lounge. These armorial bearings are repeated in stained glass in
windows.

Only 7 miles from Oxford, this hotel makes a good country base
from which to explore that large, busy city.

Manager: Jeremy Parke. *Closed:* First 2 weeks of January. *Recreational facilities:* Tennis at the hotel; trapshooting and squash a short
drive away. *Other facilities:* 2 lounges, cocktail bar, garden. *Rooms:*
19 with bath, TV, telephone, and tea-making. Suitable for wheelchair
guests. 2-day breaks. Moderate to very expensive. *Restaurant service:*

Luncheon, dinner. *Credit cards:* Amex, Carte Blanche, Diners, Master, Visa. *How to get there:* At the Headington rotary on Route A40, just northeast of Oxford, look for signs for Horton-cum-Studley (sometimes shown as just "Studley" on maps). *Telephone:* (086 735) 203. *Agent in the United States:* Selective Hotels. [T]

WORSLEY ARMS

> He goes not out of his way who goes to a good inn.
> *George Herbert,* 1633

Cricket is the theme at the Worsley Arms, named for the family of the duchess of Kent, who are lords of the manor hereabouts. The duchess's father, Sir William, was captain of champion Yorkshire teams. Old photographs of famous cricketers and old cricketing prints are displayed on the walls of one lounge, and the family arms enliven the inn sign in front of the golden stone building.

The hotel, built in the graceful Georgian period, has high ceilings and a light, airy feeling. Furnishings are a mix—some wicker among antiques and modern pieces. Food served in the attractive dining room is recommended in English restaurant guides. Roast pork with applesauce would have been our choice had we stayed for dinner. Starters included soused herring, chilled watercress soup, and cream of asparagus soup. Raspberry gateau would surely have been our dessert. Roomy bedrooms have matching floral wallpapers and draperies.

The Worsley Arms is not ye little olde rustic village inn. The atmosphere is refined, professional, and a bit reserved. Stop by for afternoon tea between 4:00 and 5:30 if you're in the neighborhood. This very civilized hotel will suit discriminating travelers.

Proprietors: Brian and Joan Precious. *Closed:* 2 days at Christmas. *Recreational facilities:* Tennis a short walk away; sauna and riding a short drive away. *Other facilities:* 2 lounges, TV lounge, cocktail bar, public bar, garden. *Rooms:* 14 with bath and telephone. 2-day reduction; reduction for children sharing. Moderate. *Restaurant service:* Luncheon, snacks, tea, dinner. *Credit cards:* Master, Visa. *How to get there:* The hotel is on Route B1257 in Hovingham, between York and Kirkbymoorside. *Telephone:* (065 382) 234.

HUNTSHAM COURT

> There are few hours in life more agreeable than the hour dedicated to the ceremony known as afternoon tea.
>
> *Henry James*

Many of the guests were gathered for tea in front of a fire in the Great Hall when we arrived. If you like hotels with a house-party atmosphere, don't miss this one. Huntsham Court is friendly, idiosyncratic, and fun.

It's a large sixteenth-century manor, remodeled in high Victorian style, a good setting for a Gothic suspense novel. Furniture is mostly antique, but interesting rather than fine. In the bar, help yourself and note what you took in a logbook. Visit the butler's pantry for light refreshments during the day. If the weather is inclement, work out in the mini-gym, suffer in the sauna, or gather a stack of books from the library shelves and sink into a chair. On good days take a house bicycle to pedal along leafy lanes.

Huntsham Court is a place for music lovers. Over 2,000 recordings, mostly of classical works (along with a few with the big band sound), are in a music library. Guests can play their favorites on record players placed in the various lounges. Bedrooms are named for composers.

A dinner party takes place each evening. Guests are seated by placecard at one long, candlelit table. Your placecard will have not your own name but the name of the composer on your bedroom door. We were Mr. and Mrs. Beethoven. On my right sat Mr. Mozart, a geophysicist from Nova Scotia. To my left was Mr. Handel, a young businessman from London. Mrs. Handel, a lawyer, sat next to my husband. Couples are separated unless they ask to sit together, or unless the Bolwigs sense that they might be shy. Dressy clothes are not required; your traveling clothes will do fine, although men will be more comfortable in a coat and tie.

Proprietors: Andrea and Mogens Bolwigs. *Recreational facilities:* Bicycles, sauna, and mini-gym at the house; riding nearby. *Other facilities:* Great hall, drawing room, billiards room, library, music room, cocktail bar, laundry service, garden. *Rooms:* 12 with bath. Moderate to expensive. *Restaurant service:* Dinner by reservation. *Credit cards:* Master, Visa. *How to get there:* From Taunton take Route 361 towards Bampton. Follow signs to Huntsham Court. *Telephone:* (03986) 210. [T]

YE OLDE BELL

> By Hurley Weir . . . I have often thought that I could stay a month without having sufficient time to drink in all the beauty of the scene. The village of Hurley . . . is as old a little spot as there is on the river, dating from times of King Sebert and King Offa.
>
> *Jerome K. Jerome,* 1889

Ye Olde Bell, pictured on our cover, claims to be the oldest inn in England. In 1135 it began life as the guest house of a Benedictine monastery, and tradition has it that there still remains a walled underground passage to the monastery ruins. The Cavalier soldier-poet Richard Lovelace wrote some of his memorable poems while under its ancient beams. Beside a blazing fire in the great fireplace of the lounge bar are mementos of more recent history—framed letters from General Dwight Eisenhower and Winston Churchill, frequent visitors during World War II, when American officers were quartered in Hurley.

Our bedroom, furnished with antiques that included a Victorian sofa, had a dressing room and overlooked a garden filled with morning bird song. A few rooms have modern furnishings. Some doorways off the twisting, narrow hallways are only 5 feet 6 inches high and bear placards that say "Duck or Grouse." The atmosphere is somewhat impersonal.

A five-minute walk through the little village brings you to a rural section of the Thames where boats and swans go through a lock every few minutes. The restaurant, with its exceptional food, attracts guests from London. On our last visit we were told Princess Anne had dined there recently and a member of the royal family had just booked rooms.

Manager: Patricia Wright. *Recreational facilities:* Golf at the hotel; riding nearby. *Other facilities:* Lounge, cocktail bar, public bar, garden. *Rooms:* 24 with bath, TV, telephone tea-making. Moderate to expensive. *Restaurant service:* Luncheon, snacks, tea, dinner. *Credit cards:* Amex, Diners, Master, Visa. *How to get there:* The inn is signposted on Route A423 between Henley and Maidenhead, not far from Heathrow. *Telephone:* (062882) 5881. *Agent in the United States:* BTH.

[T]

KILDWICK HALL

> My sister Emily loved the moors . . . she found in the
> bleak solitude many and dear delights.
>
> *Charlotte Bronte,* 1850

We found this grand Jacobean manor to be the best place to stay for a Bronte pilgrimage. It was used as a setting for the movie Wuthering Heights and is very like Heathcliff's house as Emily described it in her novel. Charlotte knew the Hall's owner, a Miss Currer, and adopted her name for her own pseudonym, Currer Bell.

From an imposing garden entrance court guarded by stone lions, the door opens into a large hall where oak-paneled walls are separated from a heavily beamed ceiling by an elaborate plasterwork frieze. A fire blazes in a cavernous fireplace when guests gather here for drinks before dinner, while they order from the menu and wine list. Besides the formal dining room in the manor, a restaurant and wine bar in the gate lodge offers an extensive menu all day.

The Jacobean bedroom, with a draped four-poster bed, original oak paneling, mullioned windows, and great fireplace, will encase you in 17th-century opulence. Another four-poster bedroom is less sumptuous, and other bedrooms have a variety of furnishings, most of them antique.

The baronial comfort of Kildwick Hall is a great contrast to the nearby stern little town of Haworth and the fierce beauty of the lonely moors that surround it, both haunted by poignant memories of the Bronte sisters.

Manager: Martin Duce. *Recreational facilities:* Indoor pool, river swimming, tennis, squash, sauna, riding, golf, and river fishing nearby. *Facilities for children:* Baby-sitting by arrangement; baby-listening. *Other facilities:* Lounge, cocktail lounge, garden. *Rooms:* 8 double, 4 single, with bath, TV, and telephone; 2-night reduction. Expensive. *Restaurant service:* Luncheon, snacks all day, tea, supper, dinner. *Credit cards:* Amex, Diners, Master, Visa *How to get there:* From Route A629 north of Keighley, turn right at the church in Kildwick, go to the end of the road. Kildwick Hall will be on the hill ahead. *Telephone:* (0535) 32244　　　　　　　　　　　　　　　　　[T]

MEADOW HOUSE

> Among the meadows of the countryside,
> From city noise and tumult far away.
> *John Russell Hayes*

David and Marion MacAuslan left all city noise and tumult far away when they departed London to entertain guests in this historic sixteenth-century rectory, set in eight acres of garden with a stream and waterfall. After we walked through the exceptionally attractive rooms, we were not surprised to learn that Marion had worked as an interior designer. The impression is light and airy—a quarry-tile entrance hall, stripped pine, floral fabrics, pretty colors. Bedrooms are large, with luxurious bathrooms and views of the Bristol Channel and the Quantocks.

Dining inside or on the garden terrace, guests may sit together or not, as they choose. The menu, which changes daily, combines imagination with culinary expertise and makes full use of garden and local produce. You may find some unusual items such as quail eggs. Choices of main course the day we arrived were breast of chicken poached in white wine with watercress sauce, fillet of lamb, and baked red mullet. David's hobby is wine. His list of over 300 varieties has won an award as the best in Britain. Smoking is not allowed in the dining room.

We came upon Meadow House one morning after we had stayed at an ancient inn that had been modernized in a disappointing manner. How sorry we were that we had not gone just a little farther to find this delightful place.

Proprietors: David and Marion MacAuslan. *Recreational facilities:* Riding, ocean swimming, and golf nearby. *Other facilities:* Lounge, drawing room, billiard room, cocktail bar, garden. *Rooms:* 5 with bath, TV, and tea-making; 2-bedroom self-catering cottage. 3-day reduction. No children under 9 except in cottage. Moderate. *Credit cards:* Master, Visa. *How to get there:* Kilve is signposted on Route 39 just east of Williton. *Telephone:* (027874) 546.

GEORGE AND DRAGON

> No more the coaches shall I see
> Come trundling from the yard,
> Nor hear the horn blown cheerily
> By brandy-bibbing guard.
>
> *Anonymous*

On a quaint market square, the George and Dragon has provided hospitality since the thirteenth century. You'll drive under an arch into an innyard where coach wheels once clattered over cobblestones. The inn's homey atmosphere is fostered by Anne and Peter Curtis and their daughter and son-in-law, Sheila and Trevor Austin. One of them is always at hand to give personal service.

We discovered the George and Dragon before lunch one morning—too early to settle in for the day. Having been disappointed with our two previous nights' lodgings, we found this inn appealing and mapped a circle tour to the coast that would bring us back to Kirkbymoorside for dinner and overnight. A fire welcomed us in a friendly beamed taproom where we talked with many English overnight guests and local residents. The dining room's imaginative menu provides a varied choice that caters to all tastes and budgets and offers a carefully selected wine list. Meticulous, well-appointed bedrooms have modern unit furniture and good modern bathrooms. From November to Easter (except for New Year's), the rate is a great bargain—just over half price, providing you stay two days and take dinner. Really to mix with the British, book well ahead for the New Year's program, which features a festive dance on New Year's Eve. Some guests return yearly for it.

Proprietors: Anne and Peter Curtis, Sheila and Trevor Austin. *Closed:* 2 days at Christmas. *Recreational facilities:* Tennis and squash a short walk away; riding and hunting a short drive away. *Other facilities:* Lounge, public bar, garden. *Rooms:* 26, 24 with bath, all with TV, telephone, and tea-making. Suitable for wheelchair guests. 2-day breaks; New Year's program. Not suitable for children under 6. Inexpensive. *Restaurant service:* Luncheon, snacks, dinner. *Credit cards:* Master, Visa. *How to get there:* Kirkbymoorside is on Route A170 between Helmsley and Pickering. *Telephone:* (0751) 31637.

THE SIGN OF THE ANGEL

> It is one of those rich morsels of quaint antiquity which
> give such a peculiar character to the English landscape.
> *Washington Irving,* 1822

In a village so quaint and picturesque that it looks like a view on a Christmas card, the Sign of the Angel is fourteenth-century house of great atmosphere, with period furnishings and fine paneling. Heavily beamed bedrooms come in odd shapes, with floors not always quite level and doors slightly askew—all assets to those who love ancient architecture.

The candlelit dining room, with open fire in a walk-in fireplace, provides a romantic setting for the gourmet cooking of Mrs. Levis and her daughter-in-law, Lorna. The main course is usually a roast with a garniture of colorful fresh vegetables. There is an inventive selection of appetizers, homebaked bread, and delectable desserts slathered with thick cream, followed by a fine Stilton. Reserve for dinner when you book your room, as diners come from miles around.

A sitting room with a blazing log fire and big chairs looked so inviting when we arrived on a rainy morning that we cut short our afternoon sight-seeing to return to it to read. Several pet cats kept us company.

The whole village, with timber-framed cottages, some roofed with thatch, belongs to the National Trust, as does its thirteenth-century abbey and manor farm. It was given to the Trust by the Talbot family, whose most famous member was W. H. Fox-Talbot, a pioneer of photography who made the first photographic prints in 1833. An abbey barn houses the Kodak Photographic Museum.

This medieval village is a fine destination for train travelers, as the inn will send someone to meet the train at Chippenham. Jaunts about the countryside can be made by local bus.

Proprietors: The Levis family. *Closed:* December 22–January 1. *Other facilities:* Lounge, garden. *Rooms:* 6 with bath. 2-day reduction; winter breaks. No children under 12. Moderate. *Restaurant service:* Luncheon (closed Saturday), dinner (closed Sunday). *How to get there:* Lacock is on Route A350, 2 miles from Chippenham. Guests can be met at the Chippenham railway station. *Telephone:* (024 973) 230.

LASTINGHAM GRANGE

Lastingham is full of charm . . . sheltered and comfortable, yet with the wildness so close at hand.
James Herriot, 1979

Dennis and Jane Wood greet you so warmly that you can't help but feel welcome in their peaceful country house. The simple entrance belies the luxury within. We were immediately intrigued by a large elaborate cabinet in the reception hall, an antique Spanish jewel chest. A Jacobean court cupboard and a Yorkshire dresser were other pieces that caught our eye. In the spacious lounge, where guests sit in big chairs talking together before a log fire, there's a grand piano, fresh flowers, books, and country magazines.

Stone niches in some of the interior walls of Lastingham Grange date from the time it was a feudal farm. Bedrooms have pretty flowered papers and draperies. The menu offers about six choices of good English cooking—steak and kidney pie, roast lamb, grilled sirloin steak. We were able to order hors d'ouvres, soup, and dessert without the main course, a nice change from too many four-course meals while staying in country-house hotels. Early morning tea, afternoon tea, and a newspaper are thoughtful extras, and shoes left outside your room will be cleaned. A sheltered terrace is a fine place to stop for a snack lunch or afternoon tea.

Beyond Lastingham, the road peters to a bridle path across the moors. Take a walk through the village, where we saw sheep and new lambs wandering about. In its church there is a famous crypt, unique in Britain, that has remained unchanged for a thousand years.

Proprietors: Dennis and Jane Wood. *Closed:* December through February. *Recreational facilities:* Riding, hunting, golf, tennis, and squash nearby. *Facilities for children:* Baby-sitting and -listening; playground. *Other facilities:* Lounge, garden, laundry facilities. *Rooms:* 12 with bath, telephone, TV and tea-making. Children under 12 free if sharing. Moderate. *Restaurant service:* Luncheon, snacks, tea, dinner. *Credit cards:* Amex, Diners. *How to get there:* Lastingham is signposted on A170 between Kirkbymoorside and Pickering. *Telephone:* (075 15) 345.

Lavenham, Suffolk

SWAN HOTEL

> The Swan is a little masterpiece, the red of old gables tumbling to leaded lights, the cream of plaster, the brown of studs. It has the soft glow of an old Dutch painting.
>
> *Hammond Innes*

With its origins in the fourteenth century, the Swan ranks among the most perfect of half-timbered buildings in Great Britain and is a pride of the Trust House Forte Hotels, some of which have been modernized much less sensitively.

The spell of history hangs over the Swan, and a more recent chapter was added when American fliers stationed nearby during World War II left their names recorded on the walls of the bar. You reach your room through uneven, narrow passages—down a step here, walk uphill a bit, now down three steps, turn, oops! mind your head! But there is nothing historic about the sleek modern bathrooms.

The blue cloth of Lavenham was famous throughout Europe before Columbus set sail to find that new route to the Indies. Immensely rich merchants built the Wool Hall and Guildhall, which still remain, as does the perpendicular church, unique for the peal of its bells and its priceless carvings. Around the corner from the Swan, in the early nineteenth century, a Miss Jane Taylor wrote a simple little poem known throughout the English-speaking world—"Twinkle, Twinkle, Little Star."

In this commodious and busy inn, the atmosphere is impersonal—hotel-like. For those who love old buildings but must go first class all the way, the Swan is a good choice.

Manager: Carl Smith. *Recreational facilities:* Tennis, riding, and golf nearby. *Facilities for children:* Baby-listening, children's menu. *Other facilities:* 5 lounges, cocktail bar, public bar, garden. *Rooms:* 47 with bath, TV, telephone, and tea-making. Ground-floor rooms. 2-day breaks; discount for children under 16 (free if sharing). Moderate to expensive. *Restaurant service:* Luncheon, snacks, tea, dinner. *Credit cards:* Amex, Carte Blanche, Diners, Master, Visa. *How to get there:* Lavenham is on Route A1141 northeast of Sudbury. *Telephone:* (0787) 247 477. *Agent in the United States:* THF. [T]

HOPE END

Gentle the land is, where my daily
Steps in jocund childhood played,
Dimpled close with hill and valley,
Dappled very close with shade.
Summer snow of apple blossom
Running up from glade to glade.

Elizabeth Barrett Browning

A romantic history has Hope End, whose most famous resident was Elizabeth Barrett Browning. The house in which she spent twenty-three years was demolished in 1873, but a few years ago, John and Patricia Hegarty, formerly a lawyer and a teacher, transformed the stables and coach houses into a unique small hotel that is their home. The hotel building is embellished with minarets and crescents. Decorating is simple, sophisticated, and charming. Big couches and modern pieces mix with antiques, a Norwegian wood stove, woven rugs hand-crafted locally, woven Welsh bedspreads, paintings of the district, and contemporary prints. Books, magazines, and fresh flowers abound.

Everyone books for the five-course set dinner. Patricia cooks in the country tradition, using locally reared meat and eggs from free-range hens. There is always homemade bread, and vegetarian meals can be provided. In an acre of walled garden, peaches, grapes, pears, cherries, and numerous varieties of apples are grown organically.

Literary buffs who don't drive can take a train from Paddington Station, London, to Ledbury, where a taxi will take them the two miles to the hotel. There they can wander over the 40 acres of wooded valley and park that Elizabeth Barrett Browning never forgot.

Proprietors: John and Patricia Hegarty. *Closed:* December through February and every Monday and Tuesday. *Recreational facilities:* Tennis, golf, and riding a short drive away. *Other facilities:* 2 lounges, garden. *Rooms:* 9 with bath. Advance reservations are accepted for a 2-day minimum stay. 2-day reduction; winter breaks. Not suitable for children. Moderate to expensive. *Restaurant service:* Dinner (by reservation; no smoking). *Credit cards:* Master, Visa. *How to get there:* Hope End is 2 miles north of Ledbury. Ask directions in the town. *Telephone:* (0531) 3613.

Lifton, Devon

ARUNDELL ARMS

> Oh, the gallant fisher's life!
> It is the best of any;
> 'Tis full of pleasure, void of strife,
> And 'tis beloved by many.
>
> *Izaak Walton,* 1653

In the garden of this inn is one of the last two cockpits left in England.
An octagonal stone and thatched building, it is now The Rod Room,
and around the sawdust ring where the cocks once fought stands a rack
for the fishermen's rods. The Arundell Arms is possibly England's
premier fishing inn. If you ever thought you'd like to learn to fish, this
is the place for you. Literally thousands of people have learned here

in three- or four-day courses or with private lessons. An experienced fisherman can be accompanied by a ghillie, and both lessons and ghillie should be booked in advance. All gear, including waders, can be hired.

But the ivy-clad inn, in the middle of a tiny village, is not for fishermen only. One of us stayed here back in the 1930s and thought then that it was the epitome of what an old English inn should be. Today the Arundell Arms continues its ancient tradition of hospitality. Afternoon tea before a blazing fire in the lounge is a delight. The dining room recommended in British food guides. One of its two bars is the village pub.

While the fishermen of the party are after salmon and trout, others can explore mysterious Dartmoor, all 300 square miles of it. Lifton is right on the edge of this land of tors and ghostly mists, *Hound of the Baskervilles* country.

Proprietor: Anne Voss-Bark. *Closed:* A few days at Christmastime. *Recreational facilities:* Fishing for salmon, sea trout, and trout from the hotel; ocean swimming, surfing, deep-sea fishing, golf, riding, and hunting a short drive away. Snipe and pheasant shoots are run from the hotel from November to January. *Facilities for children:* Baby-listening. *Other facilities:* Lounge, cocktail bar, public bar, garden, game room with table tennis, darts, and skittle alley. *Rooms:* 29 with bath, telephone, TV, and tea-making. 2-day breaks. Children under 16 free if sharing. Self-catering apartment for four people, with use of all hotel lounges and facilities. New Year's program. Moderate. *Restaurant service:* Luncheon, snacks, dinner. *Credit cards:* Amex, Diners, Master, Visa. *How to get there:* Lifton is on Route A30 about 4 miles east of Launceston. *Telephone:* (0566) 84666. *Agent in the United States:* Best Western.

[T]

WHITE HART

Hart, for thine Hospitality
Then be thine Horn exalted
Which Cornucopia flowed for me
Since at thy doors I halted.
                                    G. K. Chesterton, 1933

Spectacular Lincoln Cathedral, on a hilltop, dominates this historic city and is an impressive sight, especially when it's illuminated at night. Sharing the hilltop is Lincoln Castle, founded by William the Conqueror in 1068, and in between the two stands the ancient White Hart. Among its famous visitors, besides Chesterton, have been Edward, Prince of Wales, who hosted a dinner party here in 1927 and signed the menu.

Today's lounge was the coaching yard in the days of the great coaching age. Now enclosed, it holds an original Chippendale breakfront filled with antique Rockingham china. A collection of silver candlesticks, used daily in times past, now must be shown behind glass. Bedrooms come in all shapes and with all styles of furniture, from fine antiques to modern built-ins.

Cobbled streets lined with medieval houses, many now antique shops, lead to the lower town. The Newport Arch, marking the north gate of the Roman town that was on this site, is one of only three Roman arches left in England and is the only one traffic drives under. Lincoln is a city, and the White Hart is an atmospheric city hotel, though less personal than a small owner-run guest house. If you go, reserve ahead and ask for a room facing the cathedral.

Manager: Tino Barbieri. *Facilities for children:* Baby-listening. *Other facilities:* Cocktail bar, public bar, roof patio. *Rooms:* 51 with bath, 24-hour room service, TV, telephone, and tea-making; 5 suites. Elevator. Weekend breaks. Expensive to very expensive. *Restaurant service:* Luncheon, snacks, tea, dinner. *Credit cards:* Amex, Carte Blanche, Diners, Master, Visa. *Telephone:* (0522) 26222. *Agent in the United States:* THF.   [T]

THE CONNAUGHT

> I have seen the greatest wonder which the world can
> show to the astonished spirit. I have seen it and am
> still astonished, . . . I mean London.
>
> *Heinrich Heine,* 1826

If luxury is sumptuous living in great ease and comfort, the dignified
Connaught, which attracts guests from all over the world, is the place
to find it. Guests are welcomed by a doorman in silk top hat and white
gloves. Beds are turned down and towels are changed twice daily at this
quiet hotel in the heart of Mayfair, near famous Berkeley Square, but
the elegance is unostentatious. The public rooms have a patina of well-
bred grace and charm.

At breakfast time in the mahogany-paneled dining room, the Victorian era is recaptured. Kippers, kedgeree, grilled kidneys, and finnan
haddock are served on fine china embellished with the hotel's crest.
Many gourmets say that the Connaught serves some of the best food
in Britain. We try to have dinner there once every time we are in London. If you choose carefully from the extensive menu, your meal will
be no more expensive than at most good restaurants.

It would be difficult to overpraise the quality of the Connaught. If
you can afford it, it's well worth the splurge. But book months ahead
of time: This hotel is almost always full.

Manager: Paolo Zago. *Special facilities:* 2 lounges, cocktail bar.
Rooms: 89 with bath, TV, and telephone. Elevator. Very expensive.
Restaurant service: Luncheon, tea, dinner. *Credit cards:* Master. *Mailing address:* Carlos Place, London W1Y 6AL. *Telephone:* (01) 499
7070.   [T]

DURRANTS HOTEL

No one can tell where the West End will be next year. It is always moving to the country and never arriving there.

Augustus Hare, 1878

In the West End, behind a Regency facade, there is a quintessentially British hotel that is much like a venerable gentlemens' club. Oak paneled walls, oil paintings, leather chairs, and dignified, hospitable service contribute to its restful atmosphere. Most of its comfortable bedrooms have simple modern furniture, with big puffs on the beds.

A friend wrote to us of it, "This is the kind of small London hotel people should look for—good atmosphere, reasonable price, and convenient location behind Selfridges." Durrants is owner-managed, unusual for a hotel of this size in London.

George Street is three blocks from, and parallel to, Oxford Street, near the Wallace collection of paintings, sculptures, and armor. Hyde Park is a short walk away.

Proprietor: Mr. R.C. Miller. *Facilities:* 2 lounges, cocktail bar. *Rooms:* 93, 83 with bath, all with telephone and TV. 3 suites. Elevator. Moderate to expensive. *Restaurant service:* Luncheon, tea, dinner. *Credit cards:* Amex, Master, Visa. *Mailing address:* 26 George Street, London W1H 6BJ. *Telephone:* (01) 935-8131.

EBURY COURT

The lighted shops . . . the innumerable . . . coaches, waggons, playhouses; all the bustle and wickedness . . . the crowds . . . the print-shops, the old bookstalls . . . the coffee-houses, the pantomimes— London itself, a pantomime and a masquerade . . .

Charles Lamb, 1801

"Never will we stay anywhere in London but at the Ebury Court," say some friends we recently suggested it to. If you are the sort who prefers to be treated as a house guest, not merely as a customer, if you enjoy being called by name by the staff and asked if you've had your afternoon tea, if you like little parlors with chintz-covered furniture where you may talk to the other guests, if you will take your chances on getting a room with a four-poster or, on the other hand, getting one that is plain or too small, then you will like the Ebury Court.

Ebury Street—the very name conjures up romantic images of liveried footmen, ladies in floaty chiffon and garden-party hats, and gentlemen's clubs. That sort of Edwardian splendor is in the past, but a faint aura remains. As you walk the neighborhood streets it isn't difficult to imagine Edward VII alighting from a carriage to visit the Duchess of Duke Street. You can stroll to the neighborhood pub for lunch. It is not difficult to get into a conversation at these pubs; everyone crowds around, sharing little tables wherever there is room.

English country folk who have come up to London for a visit are predominant guests at Ebury Court, which is made up of five joined terraced houses. Near Buckingham Palace and Victoria Station, it is an excellent location for those who would like to take day trips by train to Canterbury, Eastbourne, or Brighton, and it is a few minutes' walk from the Heathrow Airport bus.

You will be happiest with the Ebury Court if you draw a good bedroom, so reserve early and ask for one. Even if you book at the last minute and get one of the smallest rooms, you may feel lucky to get one at all in this convenient location in central London. Ebury Court is one of London's best-known small hotels and has a devoted following.

Proprietors: Romer and Diana Topham. *Special facilities:* TV and writing rooms. *Rooms:* 39, 13 with bath, all with telephone. Ground-floor rooms. Elevator. Moderate to expensive. *Restaurant service:* Luncheon, dinner. *Credit cards:* Master, Visa. *Mailing address:* 26 Ebury Street, London, SW1W 0LU. *Telephone:* (01) 730 8147.

11 CADOGAN GARDENS

O . . . what shall I say of London? All the towns that ever I beheld in my born days are no more than Welsh barrows and crumlecks to this wonderful sitty! . . . such a power of people going hurry skurry! Such . . . noise and halliballoo! So many strange sites to be seen! O gracious!
                                        Tobias Smollett, 1771

If you stay at 11 Cadogan Gardens, you will find it a retreat from all noise and "halliballoo." You'll think yourself visiting a wealthy family just before the turn of the century, although the staff will be friendlier than you might have found had Hudson been in charge.

The Victorian character of the place has been carefully preserved and enhanced with period furniture. In a charming drawing room, you may write a letter at an antique kneehole desk, order afternoon tea with scones and jam topped off with clotted cream, or sit reading on a tufted damask-covered sofa before a fire. There is no restaurant, but you can have pâté and toast or a sandwich in the drawing room at any time or have a light supper brought to your bedroom.

If you put them outside your bedroom door, someone will polish your shoes; if you request it, someone else will wash your car. A chauffered Rolls-Royce is ready to drive you around London or out to the country—for a suitable fee, of course. In sunny weather, ask for the key to the private garden, which is shared with neighbors, and have someone carry out a deck chair or chaise. Nothing is too much trouble.

But you must find this unique hotel, and that isn't easy the first time. First you find Cadogan Gardens off Sloane Street. Cadogan Gardens isn't just a street, it goes around in a circle. Eventually you will see an imposing house with 11 over the door. That's it. No name—just the number 11. Ring the bell, settle into a Victorian bedroom (some have bathrooms with big, deep bathtubs) in one of four connected houses, and have a lovely quiet time. This hotel never raises its voice.

Managers: Mark Fresson. *Recreational facilities:* Tennis, squash, sauna, indoor pool, riding, boat rental in Hyde Park, and boat trips on the Thames, all a short walk away. *Other facilities:* Drawing room, conservatory, garden, laundry and valet service, chauffer-driven Rolls-Royce. *Rooms:* 60 with bath and telephone, TV available; suites. Expensive to very expensive. *Mailing address:* 11 Cadogan Gardens, Sloane Square, London SW3 2RJ. *How to get there:* Cadogan Gardens is off Sloane Street. *Telephone:* (01) 730 3426.   [T]

GORING HOTEL

> Yesterday forenoon, I went out . . . and plunged head-
> long into London, and wandered about all day . . .
> only to lose myself for the sake of finding myself
> unexpectedly among things that I have always read
> and dreamed about.
> *Nathaniel Hawthorne, 1855*

Almost an extension of Buckingham Palace, the Goring set aside whole floors for visiting royalty and its entourage for the last three coronations. All accounts were rendered to the royal chamberlain. Its visitors' book is a priceless memento of the many world personalities who have slept under its Edwardian roof—Winston Churchill, Prince Pierre of Monaco (Rainier's father), the Grand Duchess Xenia of Russia, the Greek princesses Margarita and Sophia. Trygve Lie was a guest when he was appointed the first secretary-general of the United Nations. The hotel was taken over as part of American Military headquarters in World War I.

A hotel under family ownership for three generations, the Goring has accumulated a store of anecdotes about its guests. An amusing one tells of an American bishop who was asked how he made holy water. "Oh, I just boil the hell out of it" was his quick reply.

Today, George Goring, grandson of the man who built the hotel in 1910, still runs the Goring, the first hotel in the world to be equipped with a bathroom for every bedroom and central heating. Those bathrooms, luxuriously renovated, now have nothing Edwardian about them, and the bedrooms, too, have been modernized. But the marble floors of the spacious lobby, covered with Aubusson rugs, and the decorative plasterwork on the high ceilings of the dignified lounge maintain the aura of the early part of the century. Between the Palace Mews and Victoria Station, near Eaton Square, this is an *Upstairs, Downstairs* hotel for upstairs people.

Proprietor: George Goring. *Special facilities:* Drawing room, 2 lounges, cocktail bar. *Rooms:* 100 with bath, TV, and telephone; elevator. Suitable for wheelchair guests. Reduced weekend rates November through March. Very expensive. *Restaurant service:* Luncheon, snacks, tea, supper, dinner. *Credit cards:* Amex, Diners, Master, Visa. *Mailing address:* Beeston Place, Grosvenor Gardens, London, SW1W OJW. *Telephone:* (01) 834 8211. *Agent in the United States*: Josephine Barr. [T]

WILBRAHAM

A country gentleman should bring his lady to visit London as soon as he can, that they may have agreeable topics for conversation when they are by themselves.

Samuel Johnson, 1777

"The Wilbraham? The Wilbraham! My dear, however did you find the Wilbraham?" asked Gerald Stretton, astonished. I was telling the visiting Englishman where we had stayed on our last visit to London. "But shhhhh. Don't tell anyone, or you'll never get in again if the Americans find it!"

An appealing row of joined terrace houses in Belgravia, with tubs of blue hydrangeas and bright Paris awnings at the entrance, this is where the English stay when they come down from the country for a bit of shopping. The dignified but cozy paneled lounge was a gentleman's library. Graceful stairways ascend in surprising places, and bedrooms vary greatly. Ours was small, but our friends had one that was comfortably large, so it depends a bit on luck and a great deal on how early you reserve. We were happy to get one at all when we telephoned from Scotland a week ahead.

There is no formal dining room at the hotel, but the extensive bar-lounge menu ranges from a sandwich or homemade soup with crusty French bread to a steak or a mixed grill with vegetables for a modest price—a welcome find in this expensive part of London. It's a relaxing spot for lunch if you are shopping in the Sloane Street area.

Don't miss nearby Harrods, and bring film to photograph the displays in its food halls. You'll probably see nothing like them anywhere else in the world.

Manager: D. Mullane. *Facilities for children:* Baby-sitting. *Other facilities:* Lounge, TV lounge, cocktail lounge. *Rooms:* 57, 34 with bath, all with telephone. Moderate to expensive. *Restaurant service:* Snacks and dinner, except Sunday. *Mailing address:* 1 Wilbraham Place, London SW1X 9AE. *How to get there:* Wilbraham Place is off Sloane Street near Sloane Square. *Telephone:* (01) 730 8296.

Long Melford, Suffolk

BULL HOTEL

There cannot be a cleanlier, civiller inn than this is;
which bears all the marks of old gentility, and of having been a manor house.

John Byng, 1787

About five hundred years ago the house that is now the Bull Hotel was
built by a wealthy wool merchant. By 1580, the sign of the Bull was
outside and the establishment was dispensing ale and hospitality. John
Byng, author of the quotation above, might have stopped there in 1787.

For more than a century the timbered frontage was hidden from view
by a Georgian brick front. In 1935, the 9-inch-thick brickwork was
removed, revealing a magnificent example of oak half-timbering,
perhaps the most romantic of all types of English architecture.

A huge hearth, some 12 feet wide, of Elizabethan brickwork, spanned by a massive oak mantel beam carved by a sixteenth-century craftsman, dominates the lounge. Room 30, with a velvet love seat before a tiled fireplace in an alcove, was our favorite. If the bedrooms are haunted by history, the bathrooms are not. They would suit even those who prefer new high-rise hotels to historic lodgings.

Lovers of venerable architecture will want to visit the nearby church with its beautiful old stained-glass windows, and everyone will want to browse in some of the antique shops in the town.

Manager: W. Peters. *Recreational facilities:* Fishing, riding, squash, and golf a short drive away. *Facilities for children:* Baby-listening, children's menu. *Other facilities:* 2 lounges, public bar. *Rooms:* 27 with bath, TV, telephone, and tea-making. Ground-floor rooms. 2-day breaks; children under 16 free if sharing. Expensive. *Restaurant service:* Luncheon, snacks, tea, dinner. *Credit cards:* Amex, Carte Blanche, Diners, Master, Visa. *How to get there:* Long Melford is on Route A134 about 3 miles north of Sudbury, where guests can be met at the railway station, and about 12 miles south of Bury St Edmunds. *Telephone:* (0787) 78494. *Agent in the United States:* THF.   [T]

FEATHERS

> This is one of the best towns for a gentell family of small fortune to retire to, I have ever seen for it is cheap, well built, and clean, surrounded by a charming country; and river; and affords a theatre, public walks, an assembly once a fortnight, and annual races.
>
> *John Byng,* 1784

That was Ludlow when intrepid traveler John Byng described it. He must have stepped into Feathers, a famous and ancient hostelry even then. The mists of time have clouded its construction date, but it stood there in 1521, and the massive entrance door with its 350 iron studs is the original. Renowned throughout the world for antiquity and architectural interest, the Feathers, with its magnificently ornate facade, was one of the first licensed hotels in England.

Our bedroom was comfortable with a good bathroom, but it was furnished in an uninspired hotel-modern style. Some bedrooms have antiques, including four-posters, but book well ahead for these. In the attractive stone and timbered restaurant the waitresses wore old-style dresses with white mob caps. The menu was extensive and the food good. The Feathers has the atmosphere of a city hotel where guests do not meet easily.

One of the most romantic places in Britain, Ludlow was once a walled Norman town guarding the Welsh border. Walk the same streets trod by John Milton, and visit the cemetery where A. E. Housman lies. Did the poor little princes, later murdered in the Tower, play together when they lived in Ludlow? Were they even then in fear for their lives? When the religious Catherine of Aragon, first wife of Henry VIII, was here, did she pray in the Church of Saint Laurence, where you can kneel today? This is a historian's dream town.

Proprietor: Osmond Edwards. *Recreational facilities:* Riding, tennis, and indoor pool a short drive away. *Facilities for children:* Baby-listening. *Other facilities:* Lounge, 2 public bars. *Rooms:* 37 with bath, TV, and telephone. Christmas program. Moderate to expensive. *Restaurant service:* Luncheon, snacks, dinner. *Credit cards:* Amex, Diners, Master, Visa. *How to get there:* Ludlow is on Route A49 between Hereford and Shrewsbury. *Telephone:* (0584) 5261. *Agent in the United States:* Josephine Barr. [T]

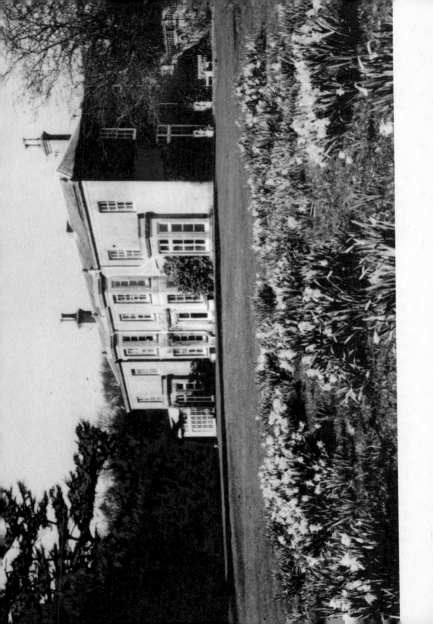

Lyndhurst, Hampshire

PARKHILL HOTEL

> One of the drollest things I have ever seen was a wild horse window-shopping for a hat on the main street of Lyndhurst . . . she was looking through the plate glass with an expression of such wearied disdain, such utter cynical disgust, that I was surprised the management did not rush out to protest.
>
> *Ruth McKenney,* 1950

The Parkhill Hotel stands in the New Forest, where landowners hold ancient grazing rights. Their horses roam freely across gorse-splashed moors and stroll with a proprietary air down the streets of busy towns. Cattle guards keep them off main highways. This quiet country house outside the town center was once a boarding school where a grandson of Queen Victoria's was a pupil and T. S. Eliot taught.

Carved pineapples decorate the building, built in 1770 by the man who introduced the pineapple to England. French doors open to the terrace from the Georgian lounge, where tea is set out every afternoon. Chintz covers on deep armchairs, old hunting prints on walls, potpourri in Chinese bowls—all convey an air so very nice, so truly English that the modernized cocktail lounge disappoints; but it is a comfortable and friendly place where, before dinner, you will meet other guests, many of whom have lived in British colonial possessions—Kenya, Rhodesia, India, Malta—most of their lives and are now back home.

Good English cooking was served to us in a pleasant dining room overlooking a putting green shaded by 200-year-old trees. Vegetables are grown in the hotel's kitchen gardens and greenhouse. Our smiling waitress said, "Thank you, Madame," every time she removed a plate.

The New Forest is high on our recommended list of places to see in Britain. Where else do you see ponies wandering casually through the streets as unconcerned as the residents walking past them?

Manager. Mr. Euan Rodger. Closed: January. *Recreational facilities:* Outdoor pool at the hotel; riding and tennis nearby. *Facilities for children:* Baby-listening. *Other facilities:* Lounge, library, cocktail bar, garden. *Rooms:* 20 with bath, TV, telephone, and tea-making. Ground-floor rooms. 2-day reduction. Children under 10 free if sharing. Moderate to expensive. *Restaurant service:* Luncheon, dinner. *Credit cards:* Amex, Diners, Master, Visa. *How to get there:* The hotel is on Route B3056 east of Lyndhurst. *Telephone:* (042 128) 2944.   [T]

We appreciate hearing about your experiences. If you have comments, suggestions, or recommendations about these or other inns, please use the Reader Report form at the back of this book, or write to us, Eileen and Eugene O'Reilly, Box 484R, Newport, Rhode Island, 02840 U.S.A.

Midhurst, West Sussex

SPREAD EAGLE HOTEL

The Spread Eagle of Midhurst, that oldest and most
revered of all the prime inns of this world.
Hilaire Belloc

At the famous Spread Eagle, comfort and history live together, for it
was already an inn in 1430, and the "new" extension was built in 1650.
In Elizabethan days the Spread Eagle was a center of much feasting
and merriment for the queen and her lords. If she walked in today, she
would recognize the timbered lounge. Except for more comfortable
seating, it hasn't changed since Elizabeth, with her court, watched
through its windows the archers and villagers in the market square roast
an ox and be "merrie." She might sleep in the same four-poster but
wouldn't know what to make of the strange comfort of its inner-spring
mattress.

The old courtyard has been freed by time from the jostling of Oliver
Cromwell's men and the stagecoaches of later days, but the cobblestones will still vibrate to the clatter of the huntsmen's horses and

the cry of the hounds on every December 26, Boxing Day. If we were to spend Christmas in England, this hotel is one where we might try to make a reservation. We would find church services in the ancient Roman town; afternoon teas before log fires, with a background of Christmas music; candlelight dinners with blazing plum puddings; drinking of the stirrup cup as the hunter's horn announces the Boxing Day meet assembling in the courtyard.

Anya Seton made the Spread Eagle a setting for her historical novel *Green Darkness,* calling it "frightfully ancient, all half-timbering, dim passages and smuggler's hideaways." As at all such vintage inns, the bedrooms vary, and there are some here that are rather small and plain, so reserve early and request a good one.

Proprietors: Sandy and Anne Goodman. *Recreational facilities:* Golf, riding, tennis, and squash nearby. *Facilities for children:* Baby-sitting and -listening. *Other facilities:* Lounge, 2 public bars, garden. *Rooms:* 37 with bath, TV, and telephone. Breaks; 3- or 4-day Christmas program. Moderate to very expensive. *Restaurant service:* Luncheon, snacks, tea, dinner. *Credit cards:* Amex, Diners, Master, Visa. *How to get there:* Midhurst is on Route A286 about 10 miles north of Chichester. *Telephone:* (073 081) 6911. *Agent in the United States:* Best Western.   [T]

Moreton-in-Marsh, Gloucestershire

MANOR HOUSE HOTEL

> The coffee room of the best class of English inns, carpeted and curtained, the dark, rich hue of the old mahogany, the ancient plate, the four-post bed, the sirloin or mutton joint, the tea, muffins, Cheshire and Stilton, the ale, the coal-fire and The Times, form an epitome of England: . . . the tea is fragrant with Cowper's memory, and suggestive of East India conquest.
> *Henry Tuckerman, 1845*

This entrancing inn of mellow golden stone, dating from 1540, is indeed of the "best class of English inns," and today, in its Old World lounges, fires still make for a cheery atmosphere in which to enjoy an afternoon tea or a nightcap. The original building features a priest's hiding hole, a secret passage, and the Moot Room, where in days gone by town merchants settled their disputes. Twisting corridors lead to antique-filled chambers—one reputed to be haunted. In the new wing, built of the same golden stone, are attractive modern bedrooms and baths. The large garden is a haven of tranquility, completely enclosed by high stone walls.

The hotel is on the High Street, which has a number of antique shops. Roman Legions marched here nearly two thousand years ago, as this was part of the old Roman Fosse Way, which cut across Britain in the far-off past. For those history buffs who love other eras but insist on today's comforts, this Cotswold hotel is the perfect place to stay.

Proprietor: Michael Fentum. *Recreational facilities:* Tennis, indoor pool, and sauna at the hotel; riding nearby. *Other facilities:* Lounge, cocktail lounge, garden. *Rooms:* 40, 38 with bath, all with TV and telephone. Suitable for wheelchair guests. Winter breaks; Christmas program. Moderate. *Restaurant service:* Luncheon, snacks, tea, and dinner (coat and tie, please). *Credit cards:* Amex, Diners, Visa. *How to get there:* Moreton-in-Marsh is on Route A44 between Chipping Norton and Broadway or take the train from Paddington Station, London, to Moreton-in-Marsh. *Telephone:* (0608) 50501.   [T]

PERCY ARMS

This deed was done at Otterbourne,
About the breaking of the day.
Earl Douglas was buried by the bracken bush
And the Percy led captive away.

Anonymous

The hotel's name commemorates Lord Percy and the famous border battle of Otterburn in 1388. Once a posting house from the bygone era of coaching, the Percy Arms today is a comfortable blend of Old World charm and New World comfort, set amid the scenic splendor of Northumberland's moors.

Deep, soft chairs before log fires mix well with old oak settles, a Welsh cupboard, and converted oil lamps. Some bedrooms have traditional painted furniture; some are modern, but these are decorated with soft traditional prints. A "taste of England" menu is added to the regular offerings in the dining room, and snacks are available after restaurant hours, handy for late arrivals or those who get hungry before bedtime. Tea in the garden is nice on a sunny day.

One friend told us her room was noisy with music from the bar underneath. When we took this up with the management, they explained that these are the last rooms to be given out, and the bar closes at eleven. So if you want to go to sleep early, make sure you don't get a room over the bar. This hotel is a convenient stop on a drive to Scotland.

Proprietors: Alice and Clive Emerson. *Recreational facilities:* Riding and fishing a short drive away. *Other facilities:* 2 lounges, TV lounge, cocktail bar, public bar, garden. *Rooms:* 30 with bath, telephone, TV, and tea-making. Suitable for wheelchair guests. Off-season rates; 2-day breaks; Christmas program. Children under 10 free if sharing, discount if in separate room. Moderate. *Restaurant service:* Luncheon, snacks, tea, dinner. *Credit cards:* Amex, Diners, Master, Visa. *How to get there:* The hotel is on Route A696. *Telephone:* (0830) 20261. *Agent in the United States:* Selective Hotels.   [T]

SHARROW BAY

> I wandered lonely as a cloud
> That floats on high o'er vales and hills,
> When all at once I saw a crowd,
> A host, of golden daffodils,
> Beside the lake, beneath the trees,
> Fluttering and dancing in the breeze.
>
> *William Wordsworth,* 1807

Some hotels are situated in glorious countryside with spectacular views, and others are beautifully furnished with antiques. Then there are those with a relaxed and cordial atmosphere, and others renowned for flawless food and service. Sharrow Bay is one of the rare hotels that combines all such qualities.

Interiors are a marvelous confusion of soft couches, curvy chairs, intriguing books, paintings and prints and framed mottoes, figurines, clocks, and wild English lamps. Sherry in each bedroom greets the guest, as do fresh flowers and luxury colognes. Each dish that Francis Coulson, the owner-chef, serves looks like a picture in *Gourmet* magazine, and he visits every table asking if all is satisfactory. Brian Sack, his partner, attends to each guest's desires with easy graciousness.

This is a very personal luxury hotel, a member of the renowned Relais et Chateaux Hotels. Its guest register boasts many famous names, among them opera star Joan Sutherland, a personal friend for whom Francis Coulson named a special dessert, the Joan Sutherland Bavarois. J.B. Priestley and Norman Vincent Peale have stayed here.

Walk along the shores of Lake Ullswater, as Wordsworth did when he saw all those dancing daffodils, or drift dreamily in a rowboat pushed off from the hotel's stone jetty. Relax over a highball while watching the sun drop behind the mountains in a blaze of splendor—from the lakeside terrace in summer or through the great bay window of the drawing room in cooler weather.

Our first choice of rooms would be in Bank House. It has its own drawing room, a dining room where its guests have breakfast, and seven bedrooms, each with a bathroom and lake views that are a treat for the eye. This old farmhouse had been transformed with exquisite taste into luxury quarters incorporating an old stone fireplace from Warwick Castle with graceful furniture, soft chairs, and Oriental rugs. We first heard of Sharrow Bay from an American who stated flatly that it was the best hotel in Europe.

Proprietors: Francis Coulson and Brian Sack. *Closed:* Early December to March. *Recreational facilities:* Lake swimming at the hotel; boat rides a short walk away; golf and riding a short drive away. *Other facilities:* 2 lounges, garden. *Rooms:* 30, 26 with bath. Suitable for wheelchair guests. Minimum 2-day advance reservation. No children under 13. Expensive to very expensive. *Restaurant service:* Luncheon, tea, dinner. *How to get there:* From Route M6 take exit 40 to Route A66, then take Route A592 to Pooley Bridge. At the church take the lane signposted "Howtown" and drive 2 miles farther. The hotel will arrange for a taxi from Penrith. *Telephone:* (08536) 301. *Agent in the United States:* David Mitchell.

[T]

Poughill, Cornwall

REEDS

Our England is a garden
And such gardens are not made
By singing "Oh how beautiful!" and
Sitting in the shade.

Rudyard Kipling, 1911

The reason Reeds is open only four days a week, from Friday afternoon until Tuesday morning, is that Margaret Jackson devotes midweek to caring for four acres of garden. She raises vegetables and herbs used in the kitchen and flowers that adorn the rooms.

A delightful widow, Margaret thoroughly enjoys meeting people and welcomes them warmly to her lovely country house a mile from the sea on the north Cornwall coast. Her dinners are a treat, as she is a wonderful cook. Reeds is featured in the British *Good Food Guide.* Dining-room tables are laid with crisp linen, silver, and candles. Pre-dinner drinks are served in the hall lounge in front of a log fire. Everything is homemade—rolls, pastries, ice cream. Fresh local fish and meat are accompanied by the garden produce. Menus change daily and guests' favorites are prepared on request. A small wine list is well-chosen. Coffee can be enjoyed either at the table or in the study, again before a fire except when it's warm. Then it might be taken on the terrace.

Three large, attractive bedrooms, some with views over treetops to the ocean, each have two comfortable armchairs and modern bathrooms. Staying at Reeds is so much like visiting a friend that you'll probably want to send a thank-you note when you get home.

Proprietor: Margaret Jackson. *Closed:* Christmas. *Recreational facilities:* Ocean swimming and riding nearby. *Other facilities:* Lounge, TV room, garden. *Rooms:* 3 with bath and tea-making. Not suitable for children. Moderate. *How to get there:* From Route A39 just north of Bude, follow signs to Poughill (pronounced Pof-fil). Do not go into Bude. *Telephone:* (0288) 2841.

PEACOCK HOTEL

> The river that runs by the old Hall's walls
> Murmured to them as it murmers now;
> The golden glow of the sunset falls
> As it fell for them, on glade river, and bough.
>
> *Anonymous*

A National Monument, the Peacock was built as a luxurious private home in 1652. Later it became the Dower House of Haddon Hall, possibly the finest stately home open to the public in England today. Haddon Hall was the ancestral home of the dukes of Rutland, whose coat-of-arms contains a peacock. Izaak Walton was a guest at the hotel and fished in the River Derwent bordering the gardens, which received a Horticultural Society award for their beauty. Today your bedroom in this antique-lover's paradise may have a high-backed bed and Gothic windows with diamond-leaded panes, but it will also have thick wall-to-wall carpets. A plaque explains the five-foot peacock perched near the entrance:

> This peacock, which is considered to be the most skillful example of ceramic art ever to be made in England, was manufactured by MINTON's LTD. about 1850/51. The modelling was carried out by the celebrated artist and sculptor of Limoges, Paul Comolera, who was employed by Minton's for a period of three years. During this time only about five of these peacocks were in fact produced. The decoration is carried out in the majolica style, being hand-painted in soft coloured glazes.

The history of this peacock is even more interesting. It was sent to Australia to be exhibited in 1878, but a shipwreck sent it to the bottom off Victoria. Some years later, when a Mr. Miller salvaged the wreck, a cask was opened to reveal the peacock in perfect condition, not a chip in it.

Manager: Michael Gillson. *Recreational facilities:* Trout fishing at the hotel; riding nearby. *Facilities for children:* Baby-listening. *Other facilities:* Lounge, cocktail bar, garden. *Rooms:* 20, 15 with bath, all with TV, telephone, and tea-making. 2-day reduction; 2-day breaks; Christmas program; reduction for children. Moderate. *Restaurant service:* Luncheon, snacks, tea, dinner. *Credit cards:* All. *How to get there:* The hotel is on Route A6 between Bakewell and Matlock, north of the junction with B6012. *Telephone:* (0629) 733518.

MERMAID INN

> The little old, cobble-stoned, grass grown, red-roofed town.
>
> *Henry James*

No one dared to interfere with the infamous Hawkshurst gang of smugglers who once caroused in this most renowned of the old smugglers' inns. Rebuilt in 1420, the Mermaid has played host to many immortals in its long history and was already very old when Queen Elizabeth visited in 1573. The Elizabethan Chamber, with a tremendous four-poster, commemorates her visit. Our bedroom was two stories high and had a huge rafter across it at normal room height. A bewilderment of corridors goes this way and that, reeking of antiquity and inviting exploration. Your fancy may hear a faint rustle—a stealthy creak of the old stairways—a presence not of today.

The dining room, beautiful with linen-fold paneling, is highly lauded. In the friendly tavern a giant fireplace stretches across one wall, a massive time-blackened timber spanning the opening. Cooking paraphernalia of past centuries ornaments the great hearth, where a priest's hiding hole is cleverly concealed. Ancient swords hang on the walls.

The steep hills of Rye must be negotiated through some of the narrowest and crookedest streets in England. Rye is so crowded with tourists in season that it is a wonder that the medieval charm persists, but persist it does. Henry James lived here for the last twenty years of his life. He was visited at his home, Lamb House, by many literary greats, among them Joseph Conrad, G. K. Chesterton, H. G. Wells, Rudyard Kipling, Max Beerbohm, and frequently by his close friend Edith Wharton. Surely most of them knew the Mermaid. After James's death, Lamb House became the home of E. F. Benson, mayor of Rye and author of the popular *Lucia* books, which have many scenes set in the town. Rumer Godden also once lived at Lamb House.

Proprietor: M. K. Gregory. *Special facilities:* Lounge, cocktail bar. *Rooms:* 27 with bath. 2-day reduction; 2-day breaks; 4-day Christmas program. Moderate to expensive. *Restaurant service:* Luncheon, snacks, dinner. *Credit cards:* Amex, Diners, Visa. *How to get there:* Rye can be reached by train from London. The inn is on Mermaid Street. *Telephone:* (0797) 223065. [T]

BOSCUNDLE MANOR

> There is a wind in Cornwall that I know
> From any other wind, because it smells
> of the warm honey breath of heather-bells
> And of the sea's salt.
>
> *Arthur Symons*

The atmosphere at Boscundle Manor is warm and welcoming, due to the personality of the Flints, who greet guests like old friends. They are refugees from the city, love their work, and have filled their country house with fresh flowers, good antiques, lovely upholstery fabrics, Wedgwood china, enameled clocks, and paintings of local scenes, some of which are for sale. We liked the stripped pine furniture in the rather smallish bedrooms.

Mary is the chef and her food is recommended by Michelin. The wine list is strong on French wines. Andrew cooks breakfast for everyone. It's lovely to have it in the conservatory, when weather permits, or even outdoors when it's really warm. A swimming pool is bordered by palm trees and has a sheltered terrace so guests can sit in or out of the sun.

Those traveling in cold weather will find Boscundle Manor a particularly good spot, with its double-glazed windows and new central heating system and insulation. Wood fires give an added glow.

Proprietors: Andrew and Mary Flint. *Closed:* November through February. *Recreational facilities:* Outdoor pool and exercise room at the house; riding and ocean swimming nearby. *Other facilities:* Living room, conservatory, cocktail bar, laundry facilities, and garden. *Rooms:* 11 with bath, telephone, and TV. Moderate to expensive. *Restaurant service:* Dinner by reservation. *Credit cards:* Amex, Master, Visa. *How to get there:* 2 miles east of Saint Austell on Route A390, turn at a small signpost for Tregrehan that is almost opposite the Saint Austell Garden Centre. Find Boscundle Manor about 100 yards on the left. *Telephone:* (072681) 3557.   [T]

STRATFORD LODGE

> Salisbury Cathedral was my first love among all
> the wonderful ecclesiastical buildings which I saw
> during my earlier journey. I looked forward to
> seeing it again with great anticipations of pleasure.
> *Oliver Wendell Holmes*, 1887

Many former guests look forward to staying again with Mrs. Bayly at
Stratford Lodge when they return to Salisbury. Hers is a very English
home.

We were told about it by an American couple who said it was the
nicest place they stayed in England. They expressed such appreciation
for the lovely home and their dinner there—delicious food served on
fine china, cut crystal, and silver—that we went out of our way to find
it.

It is indeed a charming place, especially for those who appreciate
the warmth and friendliness of lodging at a private home. Food served
is the best of English cooking, using vegetables right from the garden.
You can bring your own wine if you like.

The old house holds an assortment of graceful furniture from the
past. A mahogany grandfather clock ticks away the hours. Some comfortable chairs in green velvet are drawn up before a wood fire in the
sitting room, just the setting for a cup of tea after a day of sightseeing. Fresh flowers and books about the locality abound.

Stratford Lodge is a find, especially in a city as large as Salisbury.
Be sure to book for dinner when you reserve your room.

Proprietor: Jill Bayly. *Closed:* 2 weeks at Christmas. *Other facilities:*
Sitting room, garden. *Rooms:* 5 with bath, TV, and tea-making. Inexpensive. *Mailing address:* 4 Park Lane, Castle Road, Salisbury,
Wiltshire SP1 3NP. *How to get there:* From Salisbury take Route A345,
called Castle Road, toward Amesbury. Park Lane is off Castle Road
on the left, just past the park and opposite St Francis Church.
Telephone: (0722) 25177.

GREENWAY

> Such an old house fills an American with an in-
> definable feeling of respect . . . its central English stur-
> diness, its oaken vertebrations so humanized with ages
> of use and touches of beneficent affection.
> *Henry James,* 1875

If prizes were given for hotels that most resembled the private manor
of a person of wealth, Greenway would be one of the winners. Built
in 1584, it was just such a place until this century. As we sat in deep
chairs of country chintz and sofas covered with velvet, before blazing
fires in baroque fireplaces, we felt a pleasure that comes of being a part
of a vanished era.

Third-floor bedrooms have beams and alcoves, while one on the second floor was a half-tester bed. The lounge and cocktail bar look onto formal gardens, topiary, and 37 acres of parkland. Lunch can be
taken by the lily pond in the summer. Guests should make dinner reservations (jacket required) when reserving their rooms. This
owner-managed hotel will arrange for you to rent golf clubs or fishing
equipment. No one could help but like Greenway; it has quality.

Proprietors: Tony Elliott. *Recreational facilities:* Riding, golf, and
dry-fly trout fishing a short drive away. *Other facilities:* Drawing room,
lounge, cocktail bar, garden. *Rooms:* 13 with bath, TV, and telephone;
6 suites. Winter and weekend breaks. No children under 7. Very expensive. *Restaurant service:* Luncheon Sunday through Friday, dinner.
Credit cards: Amex, Carte Blanche, Diners, Master, Visa. *How to get
there:* The hotel is on Route A46, 3 miles south of Cheltenham. *Telephone:* (0242) 862 352. *Agent in the United States:* Abercrombie and
Kent.   [T]

Slaidburn, Lancashire

PARROCK HEAD FARM

> . . . a genial hearth, a hospitable board, and a refined
> rusticity.
>
> *William Wordsworth*

Before a hearty fire we sat enjoying drinks and good conversation with
other guests in a spacious lounge. It was on the second floor of a converted barn attached a 1677 farmhouse. Through floor-length windows
we watched a little sheep dog herd his charges a few fields away. The
white sheep all seemed to be wearing black and white striped socks, the
markings on their legs being peculiar to the particular breed. Nearer
the house, farm lads drove calves into a barn. The scene was bucolic.

Under high beams of the lounge are deep couches and chairs arranged around a hospitable hearth, some gleaming mahogany antique
pieces, an enormous straw basket for logs, and lots of garden flowers.
The fireplace wall is all stone. Next door, a low-beamed library is lined
with books, and a large table is spread with magazines and pamphlets
describing local attractions. A new building just steps away holds some
of the bedrooms, which have pale pine furniture and flowered Continental quilts with matching draperies.

Dinner is à la carte, with a menu that changes nightly and a good
wine list. Among the four choices for each course might be local smoked
rainbow trout, roast lamb with Rosemary, and brandy snap baskets
filled with homemade ice cream.

The Umbers enjoy pleasing their guests. Parrock Head farm is a very
good value.

Proprietor: Richard and Vicky Umbers. *Closed:* December and January. *Facilities:* Lounge, library, cocktail bar, garden. *Rooms:* 9 with
bath, TV, and tea-making. Ground-floor rooms. Reduction for children sharing. Inexpensive. *Restaurant service:* Dinner. *How to get
there:* The farm is in Woodhouse Lane, one mile west of the village
of Slaidburn. Ask directions in the village. *Telephone:* (020 06) 614.

THE OXENHAM ARMS

The stateliest and most ancient abode in the hamlet.
Eden Phillpotts, 1899

If you are a lover of ancient inns and turn all funny at the sight of worn flagstones, sloping floors, medieval beams, and walk-in fireplaces, The Oxenham Arms is your kind of place.

Writers such as Eden Phillpotts and Charles Kingsley have described it in their novels. First licensed in 1477, the inn is believed to have been built by monks in the twelfth century. After the dissolution of the monasteries, it became a dower house of the Burgoyne family, and it's now listed as an Ancient Monument.

Chairs of leather, velvet, and cretonne are drawn up around a huge stone fireplace in the cozy main living room. A granite pillar supports a great beam in the busy dining room. An interesting room is a small lounge where a monolith is set into a wall. The theory of archaeologists is that the monastic builders placed their house around this prehistoric stone shaped by man 5,000 years ago. Notwithstanding deep digging, its foundations have never been reached.

Smallish to average-sized, low-beamed bedrooms—numbers 4 and 9 are the larger—are reached by worn stone steps, up a few here, down a few there. Diamond-paned windows and fresh flowers lend more charm. Two bedrooms, each with private bath and having the exclusive use of a sitting room, are in a cottage directly across the street.

The Oxenham Arms is in a village on the edge of Dartmoor. The colorful Mid-Devon Foxhounds meet in its forecourt. It's unlikely a history buff could resist the lure of this place.

Proprietor: James and Patricia Henry. *Recreational facilities:* Riding and wind-surfing nearby. *Other facilities:* Lounge, TV room, public bar, garden. *Rooms:* 10, 8 with bath, all with telephone, TV, and tea-making. 3-day reduction. Inexpensive to moderate. *Restaurant service:* Luncheon, snacks, dinner. *Credit cards:* Amex, Diners, Master, Visa. *How to get there:* South Zeal is signposted on Route A30 just east of Okehampton. *Telephone:* (0837) 840244.

GEORGE OF STAMFORD

> Great rambling, old places they are, with galleries and
> passages and staircases, wide enough and antiquated
> enough to furnish materials for a hundred ghost
> stories, supposing we should ever be reduced to the
> lamentable necessity of inventing any.
>
> *Charles Dickens*

Although many old inns proudly boast a sinister past, this ancient
Dickensian inn has always retained a grave respectability. King Charles
I stayed twice in 1645, and centuries later Sir Walter Scott found it a
favorite resting place between London and Scotland.

It is probable that a part of the George was standing here in the middle of the tenth century. Thick exterior walls of what were two religious
houses that bounded the old inn are now deep inside the present hand-

some building. These were "hospitals," one for pilgrims and knights on their way to Jerusalem, the other a charity "hospital" that gave free food and lodging to poor travelers. The word "hospital" at that time meant simply a place giving hospitality. Visitors will see on their left as they enter a door marked "London" and on their right a door marked "York." These two old paneled rooms were the waiting rooms in which passengers assembled while waiting for their coaches to change horses in the inn yard.

Under the same beams where those in centuries past have gathered before the inn's great hearths, today's guests will enjoy deep, comfortable chairs and fine antiques. They can stroll on graveled walks and sit under an ancient mulberry tree in the beautifully landscaped Monastery Garden. Early-morning tea and a newspaper are brought to each bedroom. The paneled dining room of the George was one of only three outside London that the writer E. V. Lucas thought worth going to, and its renown continues. Make a dinner reservation when you book your room. Stop in for midmorning coffee or afternoon tea; drinks and snacks can be had all day. Although less personal than a small owner-operated inn, The George will give a real glimpse into the English past.

Manager: Philip Newman-Hall. *Recreational facilities:* Outdoor pool and boat rental nearby. *Facilities for children:* Baby-sitting and -listening. *Other facilities:* 2 lounges, cocktail bar, public bar, garden. *Rooms:* 47 with bath, TV, and telephone; suites. Weekend breaks; reduction for children sharing. Expensive. *Restaurant service:* Luncheon, early and late snacks, tea, dinner. *Credit cards:* Amex, Diners, Master, Visa. *How to get there:* Stamford is just off the main Route A1 between London and Edinburgh, a few miles south of Grantham. The hotel will arrange transportation from trains in Stamford or Peterborough. *Telephone:* (0780) 55171.

Stratford-upon-Avon, Warwickshire

SHAKESPEARE

> Let Beauty with the sun arise
> To Shakespeare tribute pay.

Anonymous

Imagine yourself sleeping in a bedroom called Midsummer Night's Dream, or in one named Twelfth Night, Much Ado About Nothing, or Love's Labour's Lost. The naming of the rooms after Shakespeare's plays was started by David Garrick, the revered actor, when he was a guest in the hotel in 1769. You can dine in As You Like It and have a drink in the cozy Measure for Measure pub.

With its nine timbered gables, this beautiful Tudor building, once an enormous private home, is the largest of the very old buildings in this historic town. The boy Shakespeare passed it daily on his way to school. He must have mingled in the throngs at the weekly market, still held just up the street, where we bought a blue and white china sugar bowl that reminds us daily of Stratford.

The low-beamed rooms, with vast, open fireplaces, are full of charm and character. The bedrooms are rather small for a first-class hotel, and some are completely modern; but in Stratford you won't be spending much time in your room. About 1912 a guest wrote that "it is almost a sufficient curiosity in itself to repay one for the trip."

Manager: Tim Ireson. *Recreational facilities:* Tennis, squash, sauna, and an indoor pool a short walk away; riding and golf a short drive away. *Facilities for children:* Baby-sitting and -listening. *Other facilities:* 2 lounges, cocktail bar, public bar. *Rooms:* 66 with bath, TV, telephone, and tea-making. 2-day breaks; 50% discount for children under 14 sharing (free if under 5). Expensive. *Restaurant service:* Luncheon, early and late snacks, tea, dinner. *Credit cards:* Amex, Diners, Master, Visa. *How to get there:* The hotel is on Chapel Street. From London, you can take a train from Paddington Station or a bus from Victoria Station. *Telephone:* (0789) 294771. *Agent in the United States:* THF.   [T]

STRATFORD HOUSE

Yes, he,
The pride of England
Glistened like a star,
And beckoned us to Stratford.

Robert Leighton

The walled entrance courtyard filled with flowering plants caught our eye as we walked along Sheep Street. Its charm beckoned us inside to find this small Georgian house right in the center of everything you'll want to see in Stratford.

In its attractive restaurant, which has a window wall overlooking a garden, the emphasis is on fresh food with some traditional English dishes. A small, interesting wine list offers good value.

The owner and staff assist guests in every way possible. They enjoy helping them plan tours of the area and will make every effort to obtain theater tickets, although they advise advance booking. A private-car tour service will drive guests on day tours from Stratford-on-

Avon, returning to Stratford House each night.

Proprietor: Sylvia Adcock. *Closed:* Christmas. *Recreational facilities:* Indoor pool, boat rental and boat trips on the Avon, tennis, squash, riding and hunting nearby. *Other facilities:* Lounge. *Rooms:* 10 with bath, telephone, TV, and tea-making. Suitable for wheelchair guests. Off-season rates. Not suitable for infants. Moderate to expensive. *Restaurant service:* Luncheon, pre- and after-theater dinners. *Credit cards:* Amex, Diners, Master, Visa. *How to get there:* The hotel is on Sheep Street, close to the Royal Shakespeare Theatre. From London, take a train from Paddington Station or a bus from Victoria Station. From the Heathrow or Gatwick airport take a special Flightlink bus to Warwick. Guests can be met anywhere in Britain—at any airport, in central London, or at any other place—if prior arrangements are made. *Telephone:* (0789) 68288.   [T]

PLUMBER MANOR

> The beautiful Vale of Blakemore or Blackmoor . . .
> an engirdled and secluded region for the most part
> untrodden yet by tourist or landscape painter. . . .
> *Thomas Hardy,* 1891

When he wrote *The Return of the Native,* Hardy lived in Sturminster
Newton with his wife, Emma, who called that "our happiest time."
In the midst of his "beautiful Vale of Blakemore or Blackmoor,"
Plumber Manor has been in the same family since the seventeenth cen-
tury. To maintain their inherited 400-acre estate, the Prideaux-Brune
family turned their Jacobean home into a country-house hotel.

Their friendliness and hospitality gives this lovely house a special
warmth and character. Antiques from the family collection are found
throughout, and the main staircase is lined with portraits of family
members who have lived here over the centuries. Half the bedrooms
are in the main house, all elegantly furnished and with spacious bathrooms. A stone coach house close by, reached by a garden path, was
converted to six large modern bedrooms with fine furniture and pretty floral fabrics.

Brian Prideaux-Brune already had a flair for cooking when the hotel
opened, and his talents have long since been recognized by all major
food guides. Brother Tim presides behind the bar; Richard and Alison
give personal attention to detail and service. This appealing manor is
now a luxurious hotel that successfully blends all modern comforts into
its ancient heritage.

Proprietor: Richard Prideaux-Brune. *Closed:* Mid-January to
March. *Recreational facilities:* Golf, riding, and clay-pigeon shooting
nearby. *Other facilities:* Lounge, sitting room, cocktail lounge, garden.
Rooms: 12 with bath, telephone, TV, and tea-making. Ground-floor
rooms. 2-day minimum advance reservation for weekends; 2-day reduction midweek; off-season rates. No children under 12. Moderate to expensive. *Restaurant service:* Dinner by reservation (closed to the public
on Monday). *How to get there:* From A357, slighty southwest of Sturminster Newton, take Hazelbury Bryan Road. Go over a mile and find
Plumber Manor on the left. *Telephone:* (0258) 72507. *Agent in the
United States:* Abercrombie and Kent. [T]

CLOSE

> Every step you take in such a house confronts you in
> one way or another with the remote past. You feast
> upon the pictorial, or inhale the historic.
>
> *Henry James,* 1877

Built in 1596 as the home of a wealthy Cotswold wool merchant, the Close has a richly deserved reputation for beauty and comfort. Its lounge was originally the central courtyard, enclosed in Georgian times with a superb domed ceiling. The highly lauded dining room provides an elegant background with sparkling silver and candlelight. Rooms with shell-shaped niches that hold fresh flower arrangements have Adam ceilings and display fine paintings. Bedrooms have names like Rose, Tower, and Dove, and even the beamed ones on the third floor are spacious.

While having a proper afternoon tea in the serene and sunny wall-ed garden, it is hard to realize that the front door of the Close opens onto a main street of this prosperous old town with its Elizabethan market hall. A wealth of antique shops in which to find treasure makes this a good spot for those who can spend only a few days out of London.

Even winter has its attractions, especially the spectacle of a meet of the hunt in the market square or a day at a local point-to-point. More active visitors might want to engage a horse to ride over the unspoiled countryside and then return to sit before the warmth of a friendly log fire. The Close is a fine selection for the discriminating traveler.

Manager: David Broady. *Recreational facilities:* Tennis and riding a short drive away. *Other facilities:* Lounge, cocktail bar, garden. *Rooms:* 12 with bath, TV, telephone, and tea-making. No children under 10. Expensive to very expensive. *Restaurant service:* Luncheon, tea, dinner. *Credit cards:* Amex, Diners, Master, Visa. *How to get there:* The hotel, at 8 Long Street, will arrange to have a taxi meet the train at Kemble. *Telephone:* (0666) 52272.   [T]

THORNBURY CASTLE

> Here moved on,
> In stately minuet lords, with doublets slashed
> And ladies rustling in the stiff brocade.
> *Lydia Sigourney,* 1856

Thornbury Castle's turbulent history reaches back to the tenth century, before it was seized by William the Conquerer. In 1510 the Duke of Buckingham received a license from Henry VIII to fortify and crenelate the castle. Ten years later the Duke was executed at Tower Hill after having been indiscreet enough to make some rude remarks about Henry that were heard by Cardinal Wolsey and reported to the King. Henry appropriated the castle and stayed there with Ann Boleyn. Mary Tudor lived in it for some years. She returned it to the descendants of the Duke of Buckingham after she became Queen.

In 1966 the castle became a renowned restaurant, winning many awards. For dinner, you might choose breast of wild pigeon, salmon in white-wine and orange-juice marinade, or cream of watercress soup for a first course. Continue, perhaps, with breast of free-range chicken flamed in Pernod, noisettes of lamb with basil and pine nuts, or venison and port pie. Desserts include Thornbury treacle tart, honey and almond ice cream, strawberries on a meringue with Grand Marnier, and always a fine selection of farmhouse cheeses. Two dining rooms are baronial, with paneled walls, heraldic shields, and great open fires.

Furnishings in public rooms are sumptuous. Bedrooms are opulent, with lofty ceilings, deep-piled carpets, and upholstered couches and chairs. Some have tall oriel windows and four-poster beds expensively draped with beautiful fabrics. There's a great feeling of romance to sleeping in rooms slept in by the most famous monarchs of England. They may have had absolute power over their subjects, but you'll enjoy luxury and comforts they never knew.

The castle is surrounded by its own vineyard. Thornbury's wine is included on the extensive wine list. Thornbury Castle is for the traveler who wants sybaritic perfection and is willing to pay for it.

Proprietor: Maurice Taylor. *Closed:* One week in January. *Facilities:* 2 lounges, garden. *Rooms:* 14 with bath, telephone, and TV. 1 ground-floor room. Christmas program. No children under 12. Very expensive. *Restaurant service (no smoking):* Luncheon, dinner. *Credit cards:* Amex, Carte Blanche, Diners, Master, Visa. *How to get there:* From Route M4, take Route A38 to Route B4061. In Thornbury, drive downhill to the end of High Street, take the left fork, and see the gate lodge entrance to the castle by the prominent tower of the parish church. *Telephone:* (0454) 418511. *Agent in the United States:* Abercrombie and Kent.   [T]

THE STEPPES

> One of those delightful old English homes suggestive
> of old-fashioned quiet and ancient hospitality, aboun-
> ding in antique furniture, quaint chimney-pieces, and
> the countless other relics of a bygone age.
> *James Hissey,* 1885.

Old oak beams, an inglenook fireplace, antique furniture, a warm welcome, and wonderful food are some of the delights you'll find at The
Steppes. The 17th-century house is a listed building, noted for historical and architectural interest.

This beguiling guest house is run entirely by Henry and Tricia
Howland. Their enthusiasm for their beautiful home and for entertaining guests is contagious. Traditional white plaster walls and black beams
set off red draperies and carpet in the dining room, where Tricia's extraordinary cooking is served. Praise has been showered on her adventurous menu, which includes medieval recipes served at royal banquets,
Mediterranean and Eastern dishes, and regional specialties. For those
with more conventional tastes, a full à la carte menu is available. Bread
is home-baked, and, in season, vegetables are from the garden. A fine
wine list complements the menu. Breakfast is another feast. Discuss
your dinner preferences when you book your room.

To stay at The Steppes is worth a detour to this off-the-beaten-track
village.

Proprietors: Henry and Tricia Howland. *Closed:* Two weeks before
Christmas. *Facilities:* Lounge, garden. *Rooms:* 3 with bath, TV, telephone, and tea-making. 2-night reduction. Sunday through Thursday
reduction. Not suitable for children under 13. Inexpensive. *Restaurant
service:* Dinner (coat and tie). *How to get there:* Ullingswick is a hamlet
just off Route A417, between Ledbury and Leominster. If coming from
the south, take the minor road marked Ullingswick. The Steppes will
be on your left before you reach the village center. *Telephone:* (0432)
820424.

Upper Slaughter, Gloucestershire

LORDS OF THE MANOR

Upper Slaughter . . . hidden in the complex and sinuous
folds of the hills . . . is a village after the pattern of
Hans Anderson.

J. J. Massingham, 1932

In a traditional drawing room of this luxurious old manor, there is English chintz on soft furniture, a log fire, and a wall of tall windows that overlook garden and meadow. Bamboo furniture covered in summery green, blue, and white decorates a garden room. Most bedrooms have antique furnishings, one, a splendid four-poster. On a menu that changes daily and is recommended in food guides, there is a good choice of main dishes—salmon, trout, duck, pheasant—and homemade soups, pâtés, and desserts. Light lunches that include imaginative salads can be served in the garden.

From the hotel it's an easy drive to such famous spots as Bath, Stratford, and Oxford and to surrounding villages with such melodious names as Stow-on-the-Wold and Bourton-on-the-Water. As Heathrow Airport is only an hour and a half away, Lords of the Manor would be a memorable place to spend a last night in England.

Manager: Richard Young. *Recreational facilities:* Trout fishing at the hotel; golf a short drive away. *Facilities for children:* Baby-listening. *Other facilities:* Drawing room, TV room, cocktail bar, garden. *Rooms:* 15 with bath and telephone. 2 ground-floor rooms. Winter breaks; Christmas program. Expensive to very expensive. *Restaurant service:* Luncheon, snacks, dinner. *Credit cards:* Amex, Diners, Master, Visa. *How to get there:* Upper Slaughter is signposted on Route B4068 west of Stow-on-the-Wold. The hotel will meet guests at the train in Moreton-in-Marsh and will arrange for rental of self-drive or chauffeur-driven cars. *Telephone:* (0451) 20243. *Agent in the United States:* Selective Hotels.

[T]

Welland, Hereford and Worcester

HOLDFAST COTTAGE

> This admirable region is a compendium of the general
> physiognomy of England.
>
> *Henry James,* 1875

For the traveler who values old-fashioned homeyness and good value
more than hotel luxury, this wisteria-covered cottage will be a delightful

find. Copper beech trees line the drive; garden furniture is sprinkled about under specimen trees on 2 acres of lawn and garden. Morning coffee and afternoon tea are offered there to the passerby as well as to house guests. Attractive rooms hold Oriental rugs, leather seating, Victorian bar chairs, and welcoming fires. Bedrooms are low-beamed and slanted (mind the head), all up a step here, down a step there, with pretty matching spreads and wallpaper. An à la carte dinner is served each evening with vegetables just picked from the Beetlestones' garden.

Prosperous farmlands surround this former farm cottage built more than three hundred years ago. The Malvern music festivals are close by, as are the Royal Worcester and Boehm porcelain factories.

Proprietors: Dennis and Diana Beetlestone. *Recreational facilities:* Boat trips on the Severn river, outdoor and indoor pools, tennis, squash, riding, hunting, and boat rental nearby. *Other facilities:* TV lounge, cocktail bar, garden. *Rooms:* 8 with bath and tea-making. Discount for children sharing; winter breaks; 4-day Christmas program. Inexpensive to moderate. *Restaurant service:* Tea, dinner. *How to get there:* The hotel is on Route A4104 between Little Malvern and Welland. *Telephone:* (0684) 310288.   [T]

Wells, Somerset

CROWN HOTEL

> Wells is ideally situated . . . you come upon that glorious Cathedral, set amid surely the most beautiful Close that exists . . . a marvelous spot, civilized with the culture of centuries, yet quite unlike other cathedral towns.
>
> *George Gissing,* 1894

Wells is one of our favorite places in England. Of the many old hostelries clustered in its center near the cathedral, we liked the Crown the best. It was built as an inn for pilgrims, but today most furnishings are modern yet tasteful, with antique accents here and there. There are mullioned windows and beams in bedrooms, some with four-poster beds. Try for one from which you can see the floodlit cathedral at night.

An old stone fireplace crackles a welcome in the entrance lounge, where guests can drink their after-dinner coffee. We enjoyed excellent roast lamb and broiled salmon as our main courses in the à la carte restaurant. Sautéed shrimp for an appetizer and old-fashioned bread pudding were also good choices. The friendly staff gave attentive service.

Before he came to America to found Pennsylvania in the seventeenth century, William Penn was arrested for speaking from a window of the Crown to the people below on Market Place, Quakers not being allowed to preach at that time. Every Wednesday and Saturday a market is still held there. From it we brought home a blue and white china teapot. We cherish a barometer we bought in an antique shop across from the Crown, more because it reminds us of captivating Wells than for the beautiful instrument itself.

Managers: Norman Evans and Michael Lawrence. *Facilities:* Lounge, cocktail bar, garden. *Rooms:* 20 with bath, telephone, TV, and tea-making. Breaks. Moderate. *Restaurant service:* Luncheon, snacks, dinner. *Credit cards:* Amex, Diners, Master, Visa. *How to get there:* The hotel is on Market Place in the center of Wells. *Telephone:* (0749) 73457.

Westonbirt, Gloucestershire

HARE AND HOUNDS

> And every soul is welcome
> That deigns to sojourn there
> *Samuel Waddington, 1844*

The original inn dates from the early part of the last century, and the main hotel building was added in 1928, maintaining the old style. At that time the game of polo was much played at Westonbirt, and a suite of rooms was built to accommodate a famous maharaja who played it. Dining is in the baronial manner in the imposing restaurant overlooking the gardens, which are especially glorious with flowering fruit trees in springtime. The hotel is well decorated with many antiques and is warmed by log fires.

A few minutes' walk away is the beautiful Westonbirt Arboretum, with perhaps the finest collection of trees in Europe on its 161 acres. Included among the rare trees and shrubs imported from all over the world are magnificent specimens from America. In October the maples flame as they do in New England. Walks and drives are signposted throughout, and winter-flowering shrubs ensure year-round color.

Proprietors: Jeremy and Martin Price. *Recreational facilities:* Tennis and squash at the hotel; riding nearby. *Facilities for children:* Baby-listening, children's meals. *Other facilities:* 2 lounges, game room, cocktail bar, public bar, garden. *Rooms:* 26 with bath, telephone, TV, and tea-making. Breaks; Christmas program; free for children under 16 sharing. Moderate. *Restaurant service:* Luncheon, snacks, tea, dinner. *Credit cards:* Amex, Master, Visa. *How to get there:* The hotel is on Route A433, 2 1/2 miles south of Tetbury and 1 mile north of Westonbirt village. *Telephone:* (066 688) 233.   [T]

West Witton, North Yorkshire

WENSLEYDALE HEIFER

West Witton . . . a long struggle of houses nestling beneath the hill . . . on the right is a nice little pub, the Wensleydale Heifer, where Helen and I have had many meals over the years . . . we also stayed overnight.

James Herriot

The Wensleydale Heifer was used by the cast and crew of the television series *All Creatures Great and Small*, based on the books by James Herriot. It is in his country, the setting for his delightful books.

On a crisp May morning, more like New England fall than English spring, we drove up, up, up twisting roads to find the horses at their morning gallops. The stable lads—and a "lad" can be fifty or she can be a girl—from the many training stables about, work out the beautiful animals on the great sweeps of uninterrupted lonely heath. It is a magnificent sight. We arrived in sunshine, but by the time the horses were cantering home, rain started, then sleet. Was it just the wind, or did I hear a faint cry, "Heeeathcliff"? Suddenly the sun again, and a rainbow stretched above the little villages clustered far below. This is one of our favorite memories of England.

This inn is the nearest to the high moors. In the bar it is easy to talk with local people who drop in. The attractive dining room is a recent addition to the seventeenth-century inn. The menu is extensive and the food delicious, attracting customers from cities not far away. Ask for a room at the back, as early-morning traffic is heavy through the village. Two rooms have four-poster beds.

Proprietors: John and Anne Sharp. *Recreational facilities:* River swimming a short walk away; riding and golf a short drive away. *Other facilities:* Lounge, public bar. *Rooms:* 20 with bath, TV, and tea-making. Ground-floor rooms. Breaks; 3-day Christmas and 2-day New Year's programs; free for children under 11 sharing. Moderate. *Restaurant service:* Early and late snacks and dinner. *Credit cards:* Diners, Master, Visa. *How to get there:* The inn is in the village on Route A684, a few miles west of Leyburn. *Telephone:* (0969) 22322. *Agent in the United States:* Selective Hotels.

Weybourne, Norfolk

MALTINGS HOTEL

The Village Inn, Sir, is a pleasant place
Where man finds company, good ale and grace,
And warmth when life is blowing cold outside
And that nice feeling—that these things abide.
                                        John Nicholas

In a sturdy sixteenth-century flint building, a type of architecture typical of the area, the Maltings Hotel is set near the sea but protected by a barrier range of sandy hills. It is decorated in a blend of old and new, using some antiques. The atmosphere is congenial and attentive, with such little extras offered as a newspaper of your choice delivered to your room each morning.

A large à la carte menu is presented in a dining room, with crisp white linen and fine service, that has won culinary awards. On the hotel grounds stands the original maltsters' mash house, which is now a bar and buttery, well liked by both hotel guests and those who live in the neighborhood. Salads and a wide selection of fresh-caught seafood are always available.

Weybourne is within easy reach of the Norfolk Broads, a great haunt of wildfowl, and Sandringham Palace.

Proprietor: Ross Mears. *Recreational facilities:* Ocean swimming, tennis, riding, pheasant shooting, boat rental, and boat trips a short drive away. *Other facilities:* Lounge, library, cocktail bar, public bar, garden. *Rooms:* 23, 16 with bath, all with TV. Suitable for wheelchair guests. Off-season rates; Christmas program; breaks; children under 16 free if sharing. Moderate. *Restaurant service:* Luncheon, early and late snacks, tea, dinner. *Credit cards:* Amex, Diners, Master, Visa. *How to get there:* The hotel is on Route A149 in Weybourne, between Blakeney and Cromer. The hotel will meet guests at the train in Sheringham (3 miles) or at the airport in Norwich. *Telephone:* (026 370) 275. *Agent in the United States:* Selective Hotels. [T]

SWAN HOUSE HOTEL

> I'm a Warwickshire man . . . I know the *heart* of En-
> gland. It has a hedgy, warm bountiful dimpled air. . . .
> Baby fields run up and down the little hills, and all
> the roads wriggle with pleasure.
> *Rupert Brooke,* 1913

The village of Shakespeare's mother, Mary Arden, is a peaceful place
that doesn't suffer the throngs that fill the streets of Stratford-upon-
Avon, 3 miles away. Those who are driving to Shakespeare land might
well prefer to stay here, at the hospitable little Swan House Hotel that
faces the village green. An entrance garden holds outdoor tables, a
delightful place for a snack lunch or afternoon tea on a good day. You'll
sit and look at timbered Mary Arden's Cottage, a stone's throw away.

The friendly bar doubles as a village pub where you will hear local
gossip and can join the talk. In the very popular beamed and whitewashed dining room, you'll find an à la carte menu. The hotel is enhanced by an open log fire, old prints, and a few antiques. For a combination of fine food, cheerful service, and meticulous housekeeping,
all at an extremely reasonable price, you'll be well pleased with the Swan
House Hotel.

Proprietors: Diana and Ian Sykes. *Recreational facilities:* Riding
a short walk away; tennis, squash, sauna, indoor pool, and golf a short
drive away. *Other facilities:* Lounge, public bar, garden. *Rooms:* 12
with bath, TV, and tea-making. Breaks. Moderate. *Restaurant service:* Early and late snacks, tea, dinner. *Credit cards:* Amex, Master,
Visa. *How to get there:* Take Route A34 from Stratford-upon-Avon.
Turn left at the sign to Mary Arden's house. The hotel is at end of the
street. The train stops nearby. *Telephone:* (0789) 67030.   [T]

LANGDALE CHASE HOTEL

> I had the best view of Windermere. . . I think there
> can hardly be anything more beautiful in the world.
> *Nathaniel Hawthorne,* 1854

The entrance lounge is marvelous, a great hall two stories high. Its walls
are early Tudor paneling, and a magnificent oak chimneypiece bears
the date 1664 and is inscribed "Nicholas Tufton, Earl of Thanet, and
Elizabeth, Countess of Thanet." Both the paneling and the chimney-
piece were taken from an earlier house when this stone-built Victorian lakeside mansion was erected in 1890.

Before one of the many glowing fireplaces we enjoyed the best afternoon tea we had in England: thin cucumber sandwiches, buttered toast, scones and jam, cookies, raisin cake—the lot. It was all so delectably British, with the peaceful air of another era.

From the hotel's pier you can swim, water-ski, or row. You can stay in a unique bedroom in the boat house built out over the lake, drifting to sleep to the sound of lapping lake water. Inside the mansion the rooms are a mélange of mosaic floors, oak balustrades, stained glass, tapestry, and velvet.

The grounds were laid out by the architect responsible for the Palace of Peace gardens in The Hague. Color abounds in the rose gardens, annual borders, flowering shrubs, and fine trees. From the stone terrace and cushioned bay windows there are some of the most dramatic views in Britain. Lawns slope to Lake Windermere, and across the lake wave upon wave of distant mountains seem to fall away into the mist.

Manager: Mrs. Frank. *Recreational facilities:* Lake swimming, water-skiing, rowboats, and tennis at the hotel; lake-steamer trips and riding a short drive away. *Other facilities:* Drawing room, TV lounge, cocktail bar, garden. *Rooms:* 34, 30 with bath, all with telephone, TV, and tea-making. Suitable for wheelchair guests. 2-day breaks; Christmas and New Year's programs; discount for children under 12 sharing. Moderate to expensive. *Restaurant service:* Luncheon, tea, dinner. *Credit cards:* Amex, Diners, Master, Visa. *How to get there:* The hotel is north of the town center on the road bordering Lake Windermere. It will meet trains at Windermere station. *Telephone:* (05394) 32201.

MILLER HOWE

My heart was almost melted away by the beauty of the lakes.

Dorothy Wordsworth, 1793

John Tovey, Miller Howe's entertaining host, loves to pamper his guests. He won the British Wine and Food Society award for the "outstanding meal of the year" and has received kudos from Craig Claiborne. John was an actor, and everything about the hotel is a little bit theatrical in a most joyous, friendly, and relaxing way. He told us, "A meal is like a play—every act something to look forward to." Meals here include many courses. Everyone sits down at eight-thirty each evening. The lights dim; the show begins.

The furnishings in the splendidly comfortable rooms are modern, but not ordinary—great leather Chesterfield-type sofas and chairs are prominent—but the walls and tables brim with antique clutter. The bed-rooms, hospitably supplied with not only books and current magazines but even hair dryers, cassette players, and binoculars, open to balconies overhanging terraces with stunning views of the lakeland that inspired so many of England's famous poets. Flower gardens display whimsical stone statuary.

All guests book for bed, full breakfast (bacon, sausage, kidneys, fresh eggs, tomatoes, mushrooms, kippers, finnan haddie, hot rolls), and dinner. This luxurious lodging is one that the seasoned collector of unusual hotels will not want to miss.

Proprietor: John Tovey. *Closed:* January–early March. *Recreational facilities:* Boat trips, riding, hunting, golf, and lake-fishing nearby. *Other facilities:* 4 lounges, garden. *Rooms:* 13 with bath. No children under 12. Expensive to very expensive. *Restaurant service:* Tea, dinner (by reservation). *Credit cards:* Amex, Diners, Master, Visa. *How to get there:* Leave the M6 at exit 36 and proceed on Route A591 through Windermere. Turn left on Route A592 toward Bowness. The hotel is down a hill on the right. Guests can be met at the Manchester airport or at the Oxenholme railway station. *Telephone:* (09662) 2536.

BURGHOPE MANOR

> What delightful features in the landscape are those
> old-time England homes, built in the days when
> building was a living art . . . dear to the heart of an-
> tiquaries for the histories and traditions that have col-
> lected around their ancient walls!
>
> *James Hissey,* 1889

Burghope Manor is over 700 years old and has been in the Beresford
family since shortly after it was built. Elizabeth Denning is a descendant of that family, which has the oldest recorded family name in England. By the time this oldest manor in Wiltshire came to her, years
of neglect made expensive restoration imperative.

Elizabeth had worked in a hotel in the West Indies and missed it.
She is also a very good cook. John is outgoing and hospitable. They
decided to take paying guests but were determined to provide the kind
of atmosphere friends create for friends. Says John, ''People expect
the British to be terribly formal, but they aren't like that with friends.
That's how we see our guests. These old houses have been social gathering places for centuries, with a tradition of good conversation and a
great deal of fun.''

Usually, up to a dozen guests gather in a thirteenth-century dining
room for dinner with their hosts, who sometimes invite local friends
to join in. They all have drinks first in front of a roaring log fire, and
conversation continues in the drawing room later over brandy and coffee. However, as good restaurants abound, the Dennings recommend
that guests eat out some nights. English people frequently come to relax
and play golf. If you can stay just one night, ask about dinner when
you book your room. We hope you'll be there for a dinner party, but
if your schedule won't allow it, you'll love staying in this beautiful home
anyway. Breakfast is served informally whenever you come downstairs.

Two-and-a-half-acres of garden surround the low-slung house of
pale Cotswold stone mantled in ivy. Inside is a wealth of arched Tudor
doorways, wonderful beams that include ship's timbers in one bathroom, an Elizabethan stairway, a priest's hiding hole, and enormous

fireplaces with mantels more than head high. Thomas Cranmer, archbishop to Henry VIII, was a guest at Burghope. Family tradition has it that a faint Latin inscription engraved on a stone chimney-piece was inscribed there by the Archbishop himself: "Remember the Sabbath and All that's holy. Six days shalt thou labour . . . "—the opening words, translated, of Cranmer's Church of England Prayer Book, commissioned by the king.

Surprisingly, the house is bright and airy, decorated with pastel colors. Light streams through large leaded-glass windows and French doors into a rose-carpeted drawing room. Bedrooms are pretty, with lovely floral fabrics. The modern bathrooms represent a marvelous change wrought by time.

We suggest that you stay here while you tour Bath, only five miles away. The Dennings will help you with maps and brochures of what to see. Burghope Manor offers a travel experience previously enjoyed by only a privileged few. The courtesy and hospitality with which we were treated are a happy memory yet.

Proprietors: Elizabeth and John Denning. *Recreational facilities:* Tennis at the house; shooting, hunting and golf arranged. *Other facilities:* Drawing room, TV room, sitting room, garden. *Rooms:* 7 with bath and tea-making. New Year's party. Not suitable for children. Moderate to expensive. *Credit card:* Amex. *How to get there:* From Bradford-on-Avon, take Route A363 to B3108 into Winsley, where you will see a 30 mph speed sign. Immediately after passing this, turn left onto a lane marked "Except for access." On the left is the high boundary wall of Burghope Manor. Follow it to the manor gate. *Telephone:* (022 122) 3557.

BOOTHAM BAR HOTEL

> We . . . took a promenade along the wall, and a ram-
> ble through some of the crooked streets, noting the
> old jutting storied house . . . gnawed like a bone by
> the teeth of time.
>
> *Nathaniel Hawthorne,* 1854

The Bootham Bar is a small hotel in a superb location by the Minster
(cathedral) and next to the Bootham Bar Gate of the medieval wall.
In our third-floor bedroom we were startled to hear voices outside our
window. We looked out to see schoolchildren just a few yards away,

walking along the high, ancient wall that rings the old city. Before breakfast next morning we, too, climbed the worn stone steps near the front door of the hotel, transporting ourselves into another age. A parapet 6 feet high, with narrow openings for archers to defend the city, is along the outside of the wide path that tops the wall. Below is a moat, and beyond it are the traffic and houses of the modern city. Along the other edge a waist-high stone fence protects the walkway but allows delightful views of the lawns and gardens of the Deanery and other ancient houses that were built in the shadow of the cathedral.

Centuries crowded with events have made York a rich tapestry of the past. Just think of the streams of people over the centuries who have passed through the Bootham Bar; knights in chain mail on armored horses, weary foot travelers in hose and jerkin, farmers in wooden-wheeled carts, and later the elite of the roads in the glamorous coaching age. On the Bootham Bar this notice is posted: "In olden times armed men were stationed here to watch and to conduct travellers through the forest and protect them against wolves."

The Bootham Bar Hotel has a tea room that serves light meals to public. Ask for a quiet room in the back since the street can be noisy at times.

Proprietors: John and Beverley Dearnley. *Closed:* Two days at Christmas and New Year. *Special facilities:* Lounge, garden. *Rooms:* 10 with bath, TV, and tea-making. Ground-floor room. Moderate. *Restaurant service:* Luncheon, tea, early supper until 8:00 P.M. in summer; until 5:30 P.M. (closed Sundays) rest of the year. *How to get there:* The hotel is at 4 High Petergate. *Telephone:* (0904) 658516.

We appreciate hearing about your experiences. If you have comments, suggestions, or recommendations about these or other inns, please use the Reader Report form at the back of this book, or write to us, Eileen and Eugene O'Reilly, Box 484R, Newport, Rhode Island, 02840 U.S.A.

SCOTLAND

LEDGOWAN LODGE HOTEL

> Regions mountainous and wild, thinly inhabited, and little cultivated, make a great part of the earth, and he that has never seen them must live unacquainted with much of the face of nature.
>
> *Samuel Johnson,* 1775

Everything about this former shooting lodge evokes an aura of Edwardian expansiveness. A roomy reception lounge has mounted stags' heads on the wall, all shot on the estate, and a fire on the hearth. In the dining room, three crystal chandeliers are reflected in the 10-foot-high mirror backing a Victorian serving buffet that takes up most of one wall. It's easy to imagine portly Edward VII and his cronies puffing on cigars while lingering over port wine here. Vension is on the menu when available; we enjoyed roast turkey and cranberry, served in the Scottish fashion with bacon. In a lounge full of big overstuffed sofas and chairs, 18-inch solid brass sash lifts are used to open the bay windows.

A wainscoted stair, with a bust of Queen Victoria and a stained-glass window on the landing, sweeps upstairs. One of the hall bathrooms there contains a colossal tub, which looked almost too high to climb into, and a long marble washstand. The room's pièce de résistance was the vast mahogany seat atop a flowered blue and white china bowl, a wooden toilet tank with pull-chain high above it: all in perfect working order. This masterpiece is one of a kind, however; other bathrooms are modern. Bedrooms command views of austere mountain scenery.

Graham Millard, the genial host, owns 10 acres of what was the 8,500-acre Ledgowan estate. The lodge—a place of cheerful, solid comfort, not fancy, with a warm, friendly atmosphere, central heat, and electric blankets—offers very good value in the sparsely inhabited western Highlands.

Proprietors: Graham and Sheila Millard. *Closed:* November through March. *Facilities:* Lounge, TV room, cocktail bar, gift shop, garden. *Rooms:* 17, 9 with bath, all with tea-making. Two-day reduction; free for children under 16 sharing. Inexpensive to moderate. *Restaurant service:* Luncheon, snacks, tea, dinner. *Credit cards:* Amex, Diners, Master, Visa. *How to get there:* The hotel is on Route A832 west of Garve. The train stops near the hotel. *Telephone:* (044 588) 252. *Agent in the United States:* Best Western.   [T]

LOCH DUICH HOTEL

> This day's journey was through fine wild Highland
> scenery, where rocks . . . were tumbled upon each
> other, as if by giants in a passion.
>
> *Maria Edgeworth,* 1823

After traveling through fine, wild Highland scenery, we sat in a sunny living room in a wayside inn on the road to the Isle of Skye. We were looking out at picturesque Eilean Donan's Castle, which you may have seen on Scottish Tourist Board posters. As the pub was not open, we were having a snack lunch on a tray in this pleasant room with flowered-cretonne-covered chairs. Such a cheerful inn it was, where friendly Scottish hospitality marked the service. On a windy spring day we were enjoying hotchpotch, a traditional mutton broth thickened with a rich variety of spring vegetables.

For generations Eilean Donan's Castle was a stronghold of the MacRae clan's. In 1719 it was garrisoned by Spanish troops who came to support the Old Pretender, James III, and it was battered by an English warship. On an islet in the loch, connected to the shore by a short causeway, the castle is now restored as a Jacobite museum and a memorial to the MacRaes. It is a short, pleasant walk from the hotel.

While we were at lunch, through the window we saw a van drive up to the hotel, open up, and put stairs out for villagers, who began to climb in and out. We investigated and found it to be a mobile bank, and we cashed some traveler's checks. Mobile banks are necessary in this sparsely populated land. The hotel is the center for this tiny village. A bar with a separate outside entrance is the village pub, and we were surprised to find a beauty salon on the hotel grounds. Loch Duich Hotel is a happy haven on a tour of the western Highlands.

Proprietors: Rod and Geraldine Stenson. *Closed:* November through March. *Recreational facilities:* Riding, and boat trips nearby. *Other facilities:* Living room, public bar, hairdresser. *Rooms:* 18 with shared baths; no additinal charge for singles. 2-day reduction; reduction for children sharing (free under 5). Inexpensive. *Restaurant service:* Snacks, tea, dinner. *Credit cards:* Master, Visa. *How to get there:* The hotel is on Route A87, some 8 miles east of Kyle of Lochalsh, where the ferry leaves for the Isle of Skye. Guests can be met there at the train station. Buses stop at the hotel. *Telephone:* (059 985) 213.   [T]

Ballater, Grampian

TULLICH LODGE

> To me, not the least delight of travel is the ever-growing picture-gallery of beauty spots that I gather and treasure in my mind.
>
> *James Hissey,* 1910

Tullich Lodge is a beauty spot. The nineteenth-century baronial mansion of pink granite is surrounded by 5 acres of garden and woodland that command lovely views over Royal Deeside. The rooms are furnished with antiques, fine fabrics, and flowers, assembled with style and maintained to perfection. A unique piece is the Edwardian glass telephone booth in the hall. If you don't mind the climb, there is a romantic tower bedroom with a panoramic outlook.

The food is served according to a set menu. No lesser a critic than Craig Claiborne, in singing its praises, has said that the home-baked breads were the best he had in Scotland, which, he thought, had some of the world's best breads. Roast lamb and beef are popular, and you can get yours pink, a hue not always available where meat is served in Britain. If you stay two nights and take dinner, the rate per night is hardly more than the bed-and-breakfast rate for one night.

The grounds of neighboring Balmoral Castle are open in May, June, and July, except on Sundays and when the royal family is in residence.

Proprietors: Hector Macdonald and Neil Bannister. *Closed:* December through March. *Recreational facilities:* Golf, tennis, and river swimming nearby. *Other facilities:* Drawing room, sitting room, cocktail bar, garden. *Rooms:* 10 with bath and telephone. 2-day reduction and minimum advance reservation; reduction for children sharing. Expensive. *Restaurant service:* Luncheon, snacks, dinner (by reservation), children's supper. *Credit cards:* Amex, Master. *How to get there:* The hotel is signposted 1 mile east of Ballater on Route A93. *Telephone:* (03397) 55406. *Agent in the United States:* Abercrombie and Kent.[T]

BANCHORY LODGE

Land of my high endeavor,
Land of the shining river,
Land of my heart forever,
Scotland the brave.

C. Hanley

The glory of Banchory Lodge is its setting where the Feugh flows into the River Dee, one of the most celebrated salmon rivers in Britain. You'll be lulled to sleep by the music of its tumbling waters, and in spring you can watch salmon leaping the rapids.

The white Georgian mansion, built in 1738 for the Burnett Ramsays, was later the retirement home of an equerry to King George IV. Then, as a coaching inn, it knew the shouts of ostlers and postboys. Today's fine hotel is heavily patronized by fishermen, but unless you reserve in advance and bring gear, don't plan to catch any salmon or trout.

An ideal spot for the armchair fisherman is a big chintz-covered chair in the beautiful lounge that looks out on the churning of the two merging rivers. The Jaffrays have collected old treasures over the years, including two four-posters, to furnish the rooms. Fresh flowers are everywhere, inside and out. Fresh Deeside salmon and Aberdeen Angus roast beef are specialties in the highly praised dining room, which has another fine view of the river. For year-round comfort there are log fires in lounges and bar and electric blankets, as well as central heat. The area is one of the driest in Scotland. This superior hotel is always well filled; so book ahead.

Proprietors: Dugald and Margaret Jaffray. *Closed:* Mid-December through January. *Recreational facilities:* Sauna at the hotel; tennis and squash a short walk away. *Facilities for children:* Baby-listening. *Other facilities:* Lounge, TV lounge, cocktail bar, garden. *Rooms:* 25 with bath, TV, and tea-making. Ground-floor room. 3-day reduction; reduction for children under 10. Moderate to expensive. *Restaurant service:* Luncheon, tea, dinner (jacket and tie required). *Credit cards:* Amex, Visa. *How to get there:* The inn is signposted on Route A93 in Banchory, which is between Aberdeen and Braemar. *Telephone:* (033 02) 2625. *Agent in the United States:* Josephine Barr. [T]

Callander, Central

HIGHLAND HOUSE

I always, when possible, seek out some house of entertainment conducted upon personal lines, if on a less palatial scale, and where some sort of local atmosphere is floating about.   *Arthur Bradley,* 1903

On a pretty street in the town of Callander, little Highland House is conducted along personal lines by Keith and Pat Cooper. Pat produces an à la carte menu from local produce that includes some traditional Scottish dishes, home-made soups, and tempting desserts. Keith has developed a good wine list and has about twenty malt whiskies available. This is the sort of place where many an enjoyable evening is spent in conversation around a log fire.

Although the life of the small town is but a block or two away to the left as you step out the front door, just down the street in the opposite direction is beautiful countryside for walking, from easy walks through glens for an hour or so to full-day hill excursions for dedicated hikers. This stone house, over 260-years old, will be a happy find for those seeking inexpensive lodgings.

Proprietors: Keith and Pat Cooper. *Closed:* November through February. *Recreational facilities:* Tennis, squash, golf, trout and salmon fishing, and boat rental a short walk away; riding, loch swimming, and boat trips a short drive away. *Facilities for children:* Baby-sitting and -listening. *Other facilities:* TV lounge, cocktail lounge, garden. *Rooms:* 10, 4 with bath; all with tea-making. Off-season rates; reduction for children. Inexpensive. *Restaurant service:* Dinner. *How to get there:* Highland House is on South Church Street, which bisects the main street of Callander on Route A84 between Stirling and Lochearnhead. *Telephone:* (0877) 30269.

ROMAN CAMP HOTEL

> thou shalt find
> All that's generous, all that's kind.
> Friendship, virtue, every grace,
> Dwelling in this happy place.
>
> *Robert Burns*

All that's generous, all that's kind. It would be difficult not to be happy in this charming old hunting lodge built on the site of a Roman encampment. Twenty acres of gardens lush with color and fragrance are the setting for the pink-washed building, mellowed by over three hundred years. This haven of peace and beauty, with country-house atmosphere, is in the town of Callander, a walk away from shops in possibly the most popular inland resort in Scotland.

Antiques mingle with comfortable pieces in the rooms. Of particular interest is the dark paneling of the library and entrance hall and the tapestry-covered walls of the lounge. Bedrooms offer such nice extras as fresh flowers and fruit. Electric blankets ensure that you'll be warm.

But the food here may be the main attraction. Swiss-born Sami Denzler ran a fine restaurant in Edinburgh, where we had the best dinners of a trip to Scotland a few years back. Now, under the friendly ownership of Sami and his wife Pat, the fine reputation of the Roman Camp Hotel has been revived.

Proprietors: Samuel and Pat Denzler. *Closed:* Early November–early March. *Recreational facilities:* Tennis, squash, loch swimming, riding, sailing and boat trips nearby. *Other facilities:* Lounge, sitting room, sun lounge, cocktail bar, library, laundry service, garden. *Rooms:* 14 with bath, telephone, TV, and tea-making; 3 suites. Ground-floor rooms. Breaks. Moderate to expensive. *Restaurant service (no smoking):* Dinner. *How to get there:* The hotel is on Route A84 in Callander. *Telephone:* (0877) 30003. *Agent in the United States:* Romantik Hotels.

[T]

FALLS OF LORA HOTEL

> My heart's in the Highlands, I love every glen,
> Every corrie and crag in the land of the Ben.
> *John Campbell*

In peaceful, rolling farm country where shaggy cattle graze, we found this well-modernized 1886 hotel that offers many services at guest-house prices. A lot of Victorian charm has been retained in the mix of old and new furnishings—carved tables, paintings in heavy frames, a deer head high on a wall. Through bay windows in a lounge with big floral-covered chairs, there is a beautiful view across cultivated gardens to Loch Etive. In cold weather you'll be warm in a centrally heated section where each bedroom has both electric blankets and an electric heater, and log fires glow in the friendly bar.

The accent is on personal attention by the owners, who enjoy making you feel at home. Restaurant service is varied and extensive: The dinner menu offers good choices including steak, chicken, and fish with French fries, shrimp cocktail, and desserts. Hearty snacks are served all day and in the evening in the bar.

The hotel is especially good for train travelers. Connel station is just a few minutes' walk away, and a bus runs regularly the 5 miles to Oban, from where you can take boat trips to legendary Iona and others of the romantic Western Isles. The lower-priced rooms here are an exceptional value.

Proprietor: Catherine Webster. *Recreational facilities:* Boat rental, water-skiing, ocean swimming, indoor pool, tennis, squash, sauna, riding, boat trips to the islands, and gliding a short drive away. *Facilities for children:* Baby-listening. *Other facilities:* Lounge, TV lounge, cocktail bar, public bar, garden, laundry service. *Rooms:* 30, 15 with bath, TV in some. Suitable for wheelchair guests. Off-season rates; children free if sharing, otherwise a discount. Very inexpensive to expensive. *Restaurant service:* Luncheon, snacks all day and evening, tea, dinner. *Credit cards:* Amex, Diners, Master, Visa. *How to get there:* Connel is on Route A85, 5 miles north of Oban on the west coast of Scotland. The railroad station is near the hotel. *Telephone:* (0631 71) 483. [T]

Cullen, Grampian

SEAFIELD ARMS

> Cullen has a snug, warm, comfortable appearance though but a very small town.
>
> *James Boswell,* 1773

When James Boswell toured Scotland with Sam Johnson in 1773, he found few attractive small towns. There are many more today, but the prosperous seaside town of Cullen, its small gray-stone houses trimmed with bright paint, still takes honors as one of the most appealing.

The Seafield Arms on Cullen's main street still welcomes travelers as it has since 1822, when it was built by the earl of Seafield. This fine old coaching inn has been skillfully decorated in fresh bright colors. A magnificent carved mantel that was once in a mansion takes pride of place in the luxurious cocktail bar. Chintz-covered chairs, bird prints, Sanderson fabrics and wallpapers, brass beds, are just a few of the nice touches throughout the inn. The dining room, carpeted with specially woven Grant tartan, has long been famous for regional specialties:

salmon, trout, grouse, pheasant, partridge, and Aberdeen Angus beef. Guests can have lunch in the sun on a protected terrace, pretty with white iron furniture and blue umbrellas, or in the Stable Bar, all stone and old wood.

Along the waterfront in Cullen are stone benches where you can sit and watch small boats come in to anchor behind a breakwater. A sandy beach with sand dunes behind it stretches alongside. The Old Kirk, one of the few pre-Reformation churches in regular use, is worth a visit.

Proprietors: Nick and Audrey Anderson and Tony Corless. *Recreational facilities:* Ocean swimming and tennis a short walk away; indoor pool and riding a short drive away. *Other facilities:* Lounge, TV lounge, cocktail bar, public bar, terrace. *Rooms:* 23 with bath, TV, telephone, and tea-making. Breaks; 3-day New Year's program. Inexpensive. *Restaurant service:* Luncheon, snacks, high tea, dinner. *Credit cards:* Amex, Diners, Master, Visa. *How to get there:* Cullen is on Route A98 between Aberdeen and Inverness. *Telephone:* (0542) 40791. [T]

Dirleton, Lothian

THE OPEN ARMS

> Dirleton is assuredly a delectable little place. It most-
> ly fronts upon a village green, one side of which is
> occupied by a hoary fortress of historic fame. An ad-
> mirable old inn has the place of honour.
> *Arthur G. Bradley,* 1912

The admirable old inn still faces the green in lovely Dirleton. Today it is bright and sunny, nicely decorated in a simple modern style. Most bedrooms are of average size, but number 10 is larger, with a bay window overlooking the hoary fortress mentioned above, the romantic ruins of a thirteenth-century castle.

The restaurant offers an imaginative menu with some Taste-of-Scotland specialities. You might start your dinner with smoked trout mousse or mussel and onion stew and end it with Flummery Drambuie. Room service is offered at no extra charge. Afternoon tea with Scottish shortbread, enjoyed before a friendly fire in the lounge, is wonderfully relaxing after a day of golf or sightseeing. The cocktail bar is popular with locals and visitors alike.

There are seven golf courses within three miles of the hotel that are open all year. Central heat and electric blankets will keep you warm all winter, and two-day breaks from November to May are a bargain.

Proprietor: Arthur Neil. *Recreational facilities:* Golf, tennis, indoor pool, ocean swimming, riding, boat rental, and boat trips nearby. *Other facilities:* 2 lounges, cocktail bar, garden. *Rooms:* 7 with bath, telephone, and TV. 3-day reduction; winter breaks; reduction for children. Moderate to expensive. *Restaurant service:* Luncheon, snacks, tea, dinner. *Credit cards:* Amex, Diners, Visa. *How to get there:* Dirleton is 20 miles northeast of Edinburgh on Route A198. *Telephone:* (062085) 241. *Agent in the United States:* Josephine Barr.   [T]

ENMORE HOTEL

A road might lead to anywhere
To harbor towns and quays.

Rachel Field, 1924

Dunoon is a busy harbor town, and a place from which to watch all the nautical activity is the Enmore Hotel, facing the water. Binoculars are handy on the window sill of the lounge to look out on the Firth of Clyde, the arm of the sea over which ships reach Glasgow from the Atlantic. You might see an American submarine, and your fellow guests could include an American admiral or congressman on a tour of inspection of the American submarine base in Dunoon.

Log fires, books, and bouquets of flowers enhance the welcoming atmosphere of the attractive, high-ceilinged lounge. All bedrooms, looking out on the water and down on the hotel's beautiful gardens, are varied in size and pretty, some decorated with Laura Ashley fabrics. Three have four-poster beds, one has a queen sized waterbed with its own luxurious whirlpool bath, and all have such nice extras as fruit, flowers, and terry robes.

The friendly owners here were Londoners. To get away from the big city, they opened the Enmore Hotel some years ago. David Wilson is his own chef, serving a 5-course Taste-of-Scotland dinner that includes two choices for each course. For starters, he might offer prawns in garlic butter, deep-fried mushrooms with Stilton, avocado filled with tomato sorbet, or smoked venison. Next comes soup before the main course, which could include roast lamb, Loch Fyne scallops, or pork fillet *en croute*.

An unusual feature of the hotel is the two regulation squash courts, one with video playback facilities. Hotel guests can watch the players from a bar lounge that has a glass window wall overlooking the courts.

Proprietors: Angela and David Wilson. *Recreational facilities:* Squash and games room at hotel; tennis, riding, loch swimming, indoor pool, boat rental and boat trips nearby. *Other facilities:* Lounge, sitting room, TV room, cocktail bar, garden. *Rooms:* 10 with bath; 3-day reduction. Moderate to expensive. *Restaurant service:* Dinner to public. *How to get there:* By ferry from Gourock, which is west of Glasgow, to Dunoon. From the north, take Route A815 from Strachur. *Telephone:* (0369) 2230.

Drumnadrochit, Highland

LEWISTON ARMS

Wherever I wander, wherever I rove,
The hills of the Highlands forever I love.
Robert Burns

The ruin of Urquhart Castle, medieval home of the Grants, who were chiefs of the glens hereabouts, is on the banks of Loch Ness, just where sightings of the monster are most frequently reported. Within walking distance we found the Lewiston Arms, a homey inn whose visitors are soon friendly with the owners, Nicky and Helen Quinn. After driving through mountains, we were delighted to be given afternoon tea on the back lawn. We sat beside the River Coilty, which tumbles along its boulder-strewn bed into Loch Ness.

In the little cretonne-filled lounge, residents are bound to chat with one another and with guests who come in just for dinner. Helen's cooking is so good that it is recommended in the top British food guides. There is always fresh trout on the extensive menu, but duck à l'orange was our choice after a smoked haddock chowder and prawns, all topped off by home-baked apple tart. Bedrooms are small and functional. Nicky tends the taproom, the village pub, which is entered from the street. It provides a setting for camaraderie where travelers are welcome to join in the talk.

If you'd like to try to spot Nessie yourself, walk first to the Loch Ness Monster Exhibition, where not only photographs and a model of the monster but also underwater images taken with sonar and stroboscopic equipment will show you what to look for.

This modest little inn will not suit those who need spacious rooms, but we enjoyed its fine food and snug cheerfulness.

Proprietors: Nick and Helen Quinn. *Recreational facilities:* Riding a short walk away; boat trips a short drive away. *Other facilities:* Lounge, TV lounge, public bar, garden. *Rooms:* 8 sharing baths. Off-season rates; reduction for children. Very inexpensive. *Restaurant service:* Snacks, tea, dinner. *How to get there:* The hotel is on Route A82 between Fort William and Inverness. *Telephone:* (045 62) 225.

MUCHRACH LODGE

My heart's in the Highlands,
My heart is not here.
My heart's in the Highlands
A-chasing the deer.

Robert Burns, 1786

In a hamlet on the Dulnain River, there is an old stone shooting lodge that is now a friendly, welcoming hotel. Roe deer and a great variety of birds are to be seen on its ten acres. Its rather austere exterior belies the warmth and comfort inside, where you'll enjoy the relaxed country-house atmosphere and good food. The dining room is recommended in British food guides. Bedrooms have some teak furniture.

We especially enjoyed chatting in the bar with ski instructors from the nearby Cairngorm ski area. It was early May and the days were sunny, but there was still skiing on the higher slopes. The Cairngorm mountain range is the highest in Britain, although it does not contain the highest peak, Ben Nevis.

We were tempted to rent equipment and see what Scottish skiing was like but found that the snow was very wet, which didn't appeal to us. We visited the ski area, where the lifts run all summer so visitors can catch the views from the top. It was startling to see reindeer walking about the parking area. Imported to the forests from Lapland some years back, they are quite tame. We wondered if there might be signs on the ski trails saying, "Caution, reindeer crossing."

If you can't stay at Muckrach Lodge, stop in for a bar lunch.

Proprietors: Captain Roy and Pat Watson. *Recreational facilities:* River swimming at the hotel; golf, outdoor and indoor pools, tennis, riding, fishing, shooting, skiing and ice-skating nearby. *Facilities for children:* Baby-listening. *Other facilities:* Lounge, bar-lounge, garden. *Rooms:* 10 with bath, telephone, TV, and tea-making; winter break January to April. Moderate. *Restaurant service:* Snacks, dinner. *Credit cards:* Amex, Diners, Master, Visa. *How to get there:* The hotel is on Route A398, 5 miles east of Carr Bridge and 12 miles north of Aviemore. *Telephone:* (047 985) 257.

GREENSIDE HOTEL

> A large, populous, nobel, rich and even still a royal
> city . . . the buildings are surprising both for strength
> and for beauty. . . . No blowing of tiles about the
> streets, to knock people on the head . . . as we often
> find it in London.
>
> *Daniel Defoe,* 1699

On a lovely curved crescent of joined Georgian houses, close to the American consulate, there is a friendly hotel for those seeking inexpensive lodging in Edinburgh. This convenient location is an energetic walk or one bus-stop from Princes Street and a ten-minute walk from the Waverley train station. Parking is in a metered city-parking area close to the hotel.

Terraced gardens behind the hotel are particularly attractive. They lead up into a private park that is entered only from the gardens behind all the houses on this crescent. From the park's height there are fine views over Edinburgh. Bathrooms at Greenside are all new, with both tub and shower. Some nice prints and the occasional antique piece are among the plainer furnishings. The hotel has no license to serve spirits.

Another good, plain, inexpensive hotel recommended in the same area is Belmont Hotel, at 10 Carlton Terrace, has a resident's bar and one bedroom with a private bath, but doesn't have the garden. We found this section of Edinburgh to be the most attractive area with inexpensive hotels.

Proprietors: David and Dorothy Simpson. *Special facilities:* TV lounge, garden. *Rooms:* 10, 5 with bath. Off-season rates; reduction for children under 12 sharing. Inexpensive to moderate. *How to get there:* Greenside Hotel is at 9 Royal Terrace, off London Road, which is a continuation of Route A1. *Telephone:* (031) 557 0022.

THE HOWARD HOTEL

> They have begun to build what is to be called the New Town. The houses . . . are airy and handsome, built entirely in the *English* taste; so that each family are to enjoy a whole house to themselves.
>
> *Daniel Defoe,* 1719

Three handsome terrace houses, built in Edinburgh's New Town a century after Defoe saw its beginnings, were combined to become The Howard Hotel. An imposing staircase under a glass roof sweeps up to comfortable bedrooms. Some of these are furnished with antiques, while others are more modern.

Enjoy lunch in the mellow club-like atmosphere of The Claret Jug, a bar renowned for its delicious cold buffet (except on Sunday), which attracts local business people and residents. Candlelight and flowers complement good food served in a luxurious dining room.

This fine central hotel is small enough to offer personal service and has its own parking area. Great King Street is parallel to Princes Street five blocks away.

Proprietor: Arthur Neil. *Facilities:* Lounge, public bar, cocktail bar, parking. *Rooms:* 25 with bath, telephone, TV, and tea-making. Reduction for children; winter breaks. Moderate to expensive. *Restaurant service:* Luncheon, snacks, dinner. *Credit cards:* Amex, Diners, Master, Visa. *Mailing address:* 32 Great King Street, Edinburgh EH3 6QH. *How to get there:* From the city center on Princes Street, turn down Hanover Street; go five blocks, turn right. The hotel is on the left. *Telephone:* (031 557) 3500. *Agent in the United States:* Josephine Barr.

[T]

Fort William, Highland

INVERLOCHY CASTLE

At a quarter-past eight we left Inverlochy Castle, where we had spent very pleasant days.

Queen Victoria, 1873

The quality of Inverlochy Castle matches the life-style and bestows on its guests the attention to which the queen was accustomed, but without the formality required in Victorian days. Guests gather together in the evening before fires in two luxurious lounges, where the atmosphere is reminiscent of pre-1914 country-house parties described in English novels. There is even a billiards room.

Dramatically set in the very shadow of Ben Nevis, Britain's highest mountain, the castle stands amid a striking collection of rhododendron in 50 acres of woods and gardens. Spacious rooms hold a wealth of antique furniture and Oriental rugs; masses of flowers are everywhere. Decorated with floral fabrics, the large nineteenth-century bedrooms provide the ultimate in twentieth-century comfort and offer dramatic mountain views. The dining room, which has won top honors in every British food guide, equals the quality of the rest of the castle, and the cellar includes the choicest wines. Just a few nonresident guests are seated at dinner, strictly by reservation.

Mrs. Hobbs takes a personal interest in her guests. She and her friendly staff cater to individual requirements. A chauffered limousine will meet guests at trains or airports and can be engaged for leisurely touring. Robert Redford, Larry Hagman, Charlie Chaplin, and ambassadors and other government officials have all stayed at Inverlochy. It is probably the most luxurious—and the most expensive—country house hotel in Britain.

Proprietor: Grete Hobbs. *Closed:* Mid-November—mid-March. *Recreational facilities:* Tennis and trout fishing at the hotel; riding, golf, boat rental, and boat trips a short drive away. *Other facilities:* Drawing room, lounge, billiards room, garden. *Rooms:* 16 with bath, TV, and telephone. Very expensive. *Restaurant service:* Luncheon, dinner (by reservation). *Credit cards:* Master, Visa. *How to get there:* The castle is signposted on Route A82, 3 miles north of Fort William. Guests can be met at the Fort William railway station or at airports in Glasgow and Edinburgh. *Telephone:* (0397) 2177.

Glenshiel, Highland

KINTAIL LODGE

Hark when the night is falling,
Hear! Hear the pipes are calling
Loudly and proudly calling,
Down thro' the glen.

C. Hanley

The pipes can sometimes still be heard calling proudly down the glen under the Five Sisters of Kintail. These peaks are some of the loveliest mountains of Wester Ross, and beneath them is a wayside inn on the road to Skye.

We were told by our nephew and his Scottish wife not to miss Kintail Lodge, their favorite stop on a tour of the Highlands. We found it a relaxed, friendly place that captures the spirit of true Highland hospitality. In a sprightly dining room that has red and white checked tablecloths, you will feast on homemade pâté and soups, home-baked bread and pastries. But don't think the food is simple home fare. A memorable dinner might start with haddock mousse or avocado with prawns. Then you could choose roast pheasant, Loch Duich salmon Doria, honey-baked pork with applesauce, or beef Wellington; and finish with a selection from the sweets trolley and cheese board.

A bar is also the village pub where local people come in to play pool under the gaze of an East African impala inherited from the hunting-lodge days. An attractive, homey lounge, with plenty of books and magazines about, adjoins a comfortable cocktail bar that stocks over 50 different Scottish whiskies. Bedrooms are furnished in different styles, color-coordinated with pretty wallpapers, wall-to-wall carpeting, and Continental quilts.

In summer you can take a rowboat or canoe right from the hotel to glide along the waters of Loch Duich. On brisk autumn days, explore the hill paths used by Highlands shepherds, then return to afternoon tea. This is an especially good choice for those traveling off-season when many hotels in the remote Western Highlands are closed. After you leave Scotland, you'll want to come back again—back to this lonely glen and back to the cheerful atmosphere of Kintail Lodge.

Proprietors: Stuart and Margaret Henderson. *Recreational facilities:* Boat rental at the hotel; sea fishing and boat trips a short drive away. *Other facilities:* Lounge, library, cocktail bar, public bar, laundry, garden. *Rooms:* 11, 7 with bath; all with TV. 2-day minimum advance reservation in season. Off-season rates; reduction for children under 9 sharing. Inexpensive to moderate. *Restaurant service:* Early and late snacks, tea, dinner. *Credit cards:* Master, Visa. *How to get there:* The hotel is on Route A87 at the end of Loch Duich between Kyle of Lochalsh and Fort William. *Telephone:* (059) 981 275.

Gullane, Lothian

GREYWALLS

> The ornament of a house is the friends who frequent it.
>
> *Ralph Waldo Emerson*

The register of exquisite Greywalls reads like *Who's Who*. Edward VII was a guest when it was still a private home, but since the hotel opened in 1948 the guest list has continued to be star-studded. Princess

Margaret has come, as have Jack Nicklaus, Lee Trevino, Arnold Palmer, Christopher Lee, Brigitte Bardot, Andy Williams, and Yehudi Menuhin, to name a few. Guests return over and over again.

The house was designed in 1901 by the famous English architect Sir Edwin Lutyens, who said it was his favorite. Gardens were designed by the equally famous Gertrude Jekyll. Some rooms overlook the Muirfield golf course, where the British Open was played in 1980, but even better are those looking out to a walled rose garden. Furniture is original, with a wealth of antiques; extravagant bouquets are everywhere. If King Edward returned to the library he would find everything much as he left it—leatherbound books, a grand piano, Oriental rugs, big down-filled chairs. But the modern bathrooms now fitted into every possible space would be unfamiliar to him; the whole of the splendid mansion originally contained only one.

Greywalls is luxurious but not intimidating. Giles and Ros Weaver set the style for the friendly atmosphere; the staff is smiling, kind, and efficient, and guests feel very much at ease. Some people say that Greywalls serves the best food of any hotel in Britain. Those who love understated elegance will enjoy it here at one of Britain's loveliest country hotels.

Proprietors: Giles and Ros Weaver. *Closed:* November through March. *Recreational facilities:* Tennis and putting green at the hotel; outdoor pool, ocean swimming, squash, golf, boat rental, and boat trips a short drive away. *Facilities for children:* Baby-listening. *Other facilities:* Drawing room, library, sun parlor, cocktail bar, garden. *Rooms:* 23 with bath, TV, and telephone. Ground-floor rooms. Off-season rates; discount for children sharing (free if under 3). Very expensive. *Restaurant service:* Luncheon and snacks all day and evening; tea; dinner (coat and tie). *Credit cards:* Amex, Master, Visa. *How to get there:* Take Route A1 south from Edinburgh, then Route A198 toward North Berwick. The hotel is signposted in Gullane, just 40 minutes from central Edinburgh. *Telephone:* (0620) 842 144. *Agent in the United States:* Abercrombie and Kent. [T]

BROWNS' HOTEL

Hail ye small sweet courtesies of life, for smooth do
ye make the road of it.

Laurence Sterne, 1768

"A classy place with very good food." That's the way our Scottish niece
described Browns' Hotel to us. She was right. This town hotel is an
endearing mixture of elegance and coziness within. The house, in a resi-
dential area and with lovely gardens, was built in 1810 in Georgian style.
Light streams through the glass dome of a cupola over the winding staircase. The house is decorated with strong colors in unusual combina-
tions, put together with flair and good taste. Bedrooms are supremely
comfortable, and bathrooms are streamlined.

Antiques combine with thick wall-to-wall carpet, and what isn't antique is very nice. Colin Brown does all the cooking in this appealing
hotel he and his partner run so well. The set menu changes daily. It is
so well thought of by local residents that you should reserve for your
dinner when you engage your room, or the small dining room could
be unable to seat you.

The royal burgh of Haddington is a pleasant small town in one of
the most prosperous farming areas of Scotland. It's a golfer's paradise
with fourteen courses within a twenty-minute drive. John Knox, who
founded the Presbyterian Church, was probably born here.

Proprietors: Colin Brown and Alex McCallam. *Closed:* November
1–15. *Recreational facilities:* Indoor pool and squash a short walk away;
ocean swimming, tennis, riding, and golf a short drive away. *Other facilities:* Lounge, cocktail lounge, garden. *Rooms:* 6 with bath, telephone, TV, and tea-making. Moderate. *Restaurant service:* Dinner (by
reservation). *How to get there:* Browns' Hotel is on West Road, the
main road into Haddington off Route A1 from Edinburgh. *Telephone:*
(062 082) 2254. [T]

CULLODEN HOUSE HOTEL

> Culloden, alone of all the battle-fields known to me,
> is still drenched with the melancholy of its associa-
> tion: it is the only battle-field I know which contains
> the graves of the fallen, buried in trenches as they died.
> *H.V. Morton,* 1929

This remarkably beautiful Adam-style mansion, built in 1772, stands within forty acres of parkland beside the battlefield of Culloden. It is said that Bonnie Prince Charlie spent the night before the battle in the castle that then occupied this site.

Behind the classical stone facade, lofty rooms with ornate plaster-work ceilings are furnished with antiques. Candles lend a soft glow to the high-ceilinged dining room, resplendent with silver, linen, and fresh flowers, that has an established reputation for good food. Bedrooms, some with four-posters, are large and well appointed, most with views over the surrounding hills. Bathrooms are modern, some even sporting Jacuzzi baths.

We've learned much Scottish history during our visits to the Visitor Centre and Museum of Culloden, which has an audiovisual exhibit. The moor itself is at once romantic and tragic, haunted by the memory of the terrible battle that crushed Gaelic Scotland's hopes forever. Simple headstones over mass graves bear individual clan names.

Proprietors: Ian and Marjory McKenzie. *Recreational facilities:* Tennis, sauna, and solarium at the hotel. Riding nearby. Fishing, shooting, and deer-stalking arranged. *Other facilities:* Lounge, library, cocktail bar, garden. *Rooms:* 20 with bath, telephone, and TV. Very expensive. *Restaurant service:* Luncheon snacks, tea, dinner. *Credit cards:* Amex, Diners, Master, Visa. *How to get there:* The hotel is 3 miles northeast of Inverness off Route A96. *Telephone:* (0463) 790461. *Agent in the United States:* Scott Calder.   [T]

DUNAIN PARK

> Inverness . . . has the appearance of having been found-
> ed by a member of the Royal Academy in a landscape
> mood. . . . Inverness is . . . romantic.
>
> *H. V. Morton,* 1930

Dunain Park is a hotel of character where people talk to each other.
The Nicolls make every effort to assure guests a memorable stay. The
dining room is established as one of Scotland's finest, so book for dinner when you reserve a room. Regional specialties served include prime
Scottish beef and lamb, pheasant, venison, grouse, salmon, and lobster.
Vegetables are picked almost within minutes of being cooked, and eggs
are from free-ranging hens raised on the park's 6 acres of garden and
woodland. Bread, cake, and cookies are home-baked.

Outside are horses, cows, and dogs, as well as badminton, croquet,
and a greenhouse. You can bask in the sun on a lawn chair as you gaze
across fields to distant hills beyond the Caledonian Canal. Inside are
books, magazines, games, cards, and a roaring fire. Rooms are splendidly comfortable, filled with leather Chesterfields, wing chairs, marble mantels, and oil paintings. Some bedrooms have four-poster or half-
tester beds.

Dunain Park, a place in which to stay a few days, is between two
of Scotland's greatest attractions—Culloden Moor, where Scottish
history was rewritten forever, and Loch Ness, of monster fame. Fishing,
shooting, or stalking should be planned ahead. If you can't stay, stop
in for morning coffee or afternoon tea, served with Ann's homemade
shortbread.

Proprietors: Ann and Edward Nicoll. *&Recreational facilities:* Indoor pool and sauna at hotel; ocean, lake, and river swimming, tennis, riding, golf, salmon and trout fishing, grouse and deer shooting,
boat rental, and boat trips on Loch Ness a short drive away. *Other facilities:* Drawing room, lounge, garden, laundry service. *Rooms:* 6 with
bath, telephone, and TV; 2 suites; 2 self-catering cottages. Off-season
rates. Expensive. *Restaurant service (no smoking):* Luncheon, snacks,
tea, dinner. *How to get there:* The hotel is signposted on Route A82,
1 mile southwest of Inverness. Guests can be met at the Inverness railway station or airport. Car rental can be arranged. *Telephone:* (0463)
230512.   [T]

Kincraig, Highland

OSSIAN

> Oh for the crags that are wild and majestic!
> *Lord Byron*

The Ossian is easy to reach but seems isolated. A cheerful guest house where true Scottish hospitality marks the friendly service, it's a solid stone building furnished with many antiques and warm wall-to-wall carpets. Bedrooms are all different; one has an oak suite with an elaborate ceiling-high headboard. Others command a view of the granite domes of the Cairngorms, as do the bay windows of the living room and the rustic seating in the garden. A family chef prepares à la carte meals, with wine if you wish. There is also a tea and craft shop where you can stop for morning coffee or afternoon tea. Scones and cakes are home baked.

For anyone interested in trying a new sport, this area has it all. Besides skiing, there are courses in salmon and trout fishing, a canoeing and sailing school, beginners' lessons in rock climbing, horseback riding, gliding, even the Scottish game of curling. You can rent ice skates or ski all summer on a snowless practice slope.

If you check the rates at the Ossian, you'll see that it gives very good value. You'll find it a happy haven, the sort of place where you'll make new friends.

Proprietors: Lynn and John Rainbow and Marion and John Ramage. *Closed:* November and January. *Recreational facilities:* Lake and river swimming, game fishing, boat rental, wind surfing and boat trips a short walk away; indoor pool, tennis, squash, skiing, riding, ice-skating, and golf a short drive away. *Other facilities:* Lounge, TV lounge, garden. *Rooms:* 9 sharing baths. 1-week minimum advance reservation in August. Discount for children under 13. Inexpensive. *Restaurant service:* Snacks, tea, supper, dinner. *Credit cards:* Master, Visa. *How to get there:* The Ossian is signposted in the village of Kincraig, which is off the Scenic Route B9152 between Aviemore and Kingussie. Guests can be met at a railway station in Aviemore or Kingussie. *Telephone:* (05404) 242.

OSPREY HOTEL

> In Heav'n itself I'll ask no more
> Than just a Highland welcome.
>
> *Robert Burns*

You'll receive a Highland welcome at the Osprey, and you'll find outstanding cooking. A British food guide judged it to have the best food in Scotland.

Prime Scottish beef, lamb, free-range chickens, are stars of the menu, along with salmon and trout from local rivers, outstanding whether fresh or peat-smoked. All desserts are baked right in the kitchen. Breakfast specialties include Scottish oatmeal porridge, oak-smoked haddocks and kippers, local heather honey, as well as fresh eggs, bacon, and freshly ground coffee. Few small establishments have a cellar like the one at the Osprey. It features more than 200 wines, ranging from excellent inexpensive house wines to superb clarets, all at good value. The hotel is nicely furnished with many antiques and offers electric blankets and heated towel bars to keep you cozy.

At nearby Loch Garten Nature Reserve, ospreys, extinct in Scotland for many years, returned to breed in 1959. Their treetop eyrie may be viewed through fixed binoculars from the Observation Hut.

Because Kingussie is one of the most central villages in Scotland, with a train station just 200 yards from the hotel, the Osprey is a good base for sightseeing in many directions.

Proprietors: Duncan and Pauline Reeves. *Closed:* November and December. *Recreational facilities:* River swimming, tennis, golf, riding, and salmon and trout fishing a walk away. *Facilities for children:* Baby-listening. *Other facilities:* Lounge, TV lounge. *Rooms:* 8, 5 with bath. Off-season rate; reduction for children. Inexpensive to moderate. *Restaurant service:* Tea, dinner. *Credit cards:* Amex, Diners, Master, Visa. *How to get there:* The hotel is just off Route A9 in Kingussie village. The train station is near the hotel. *Telephone:* (05402) 510.

Ledaig, Strathclyde

ISLE OF ERISKA

> O 'tis a delicious retreat both from its beauty, and air
> of solitude; and so sweetly does everything ab^t it invit
> y^r mind to rest from its labours and be at peace with
> itself and the world.
>
> *Laurence Sterne,* 1768

The Isle of Eriska has so much to recommend it that it's hard to know where to start. Most important, perhaps, is the house-party atmosphere of great warmth and friendliness that initiates with the owners, Robin and Sheena Buchanan-Smith. They are around each evening before dinner chatting with guests and introducing them to each other.

The hotel, a turreted, towered, and bay-windowed Victorian baronial mansion, is set romantically on its own 300-acre island in the Firth of Lorn. Wildlife abounds to give the place the air of a natural sanctuary; roe deer, badgers, herons, and even an occasional golden eagle can be observed. Rhododendron, azaleas, daffodils and bluebells add their beauty. Much of the hotel's food served is right from the estate—milk and cream from a Jersey herd, eggs from free-range hens, vegetables and berries from the garden. Sheena, a Cordon Bleu cook, sets high standards for the kitchen. Breakfast is hearty: bacon, eggs, kidneys, and porridge buffet-style under silver domes; quantities of good coffee and tea; hot toast and homebaked brown bread with home-made marmalades. All guests book for the set dinner (coat and tie, please) that might start with smoked haddock mousse, continue with soup followed by a choice of meat or fish and garden vegetables and a selection of desserts (try the fruit tarts with heavy cream), and finish off with a grand cheese board. The wine list is very well chosen. Morning coffee and afternoon tea are served to house guests in the lounge at no charge.

Public rooms are full of character—beautiful Oriental rugs, wood-paneled walls, floral chintz, brown leather, huge piles of logs beside open hearths, books, magazines. Most bedrooms have antique furniture and all have good reading lights, fruit, flowers, sewing kits, and modern bathrooms with heated towel-bars. Facilities for wheel-chair guests are exceptional.

Proprietors: Robin and Sheena Buchanan-Smith. *Closed:* November through February. *Recreational facilities:* Tennis, loch swimming (very cold), and riding at the hotel; golf and boat trips a short drive away. *Facilities for children:* Baby-listening, children's supper, pony. *Other facilities:* Drawing room, lounge, library, cocktail bar, garden. *Rooms:* 16 with bath, telephones, and TV. Suitable for wheelchair guests. 2-day minimum advance reservations; spring breaks; discount for children sharing. Very expensive. *Restaurant service:* Luncheon, dinner by reservation. *Credit cards:* Amex, Diners, Master, Visa. *How to get there:* Isle of Eriska is signposted on Route A828 north of Ledaig, which is between Ballachulish and Connell. Guests can be met at the Connell railway station or airport. *Telephone:* (0631 72) 371. *Agent in the United States:* Josephine Barr.   [T]

Lockerbie, Dumfries and Galloway

DRYFESDALE HOTEL

All my life long I had longed to see heather
In the land of my kinsmen far over the sea.
Marguerite Wilkinson, 1920

The Dryfesdale Hotel offers a warm welcome to those entering Scotland. An eighteenth-century former manse, its window-walled sunroom, added forty years ago, commands a panoramic view of the rolling farmland of the Border country.

Log fires enhance an appealing lounge furnished with traditional and antique pieces. There are hunting prints and stags' heads in the attractive bar. Good food is served in the dining room, and a gracious winding stairway leads to bedrooms that are on the small side.

Although it is within sight of a main road that links Scotland and England, the Dryfesdale Hotel stands quiet and peaceful on 7 acres. Its convenient location makes it a fine place for a first night's stay in the land of the heather.

Proprietors: James and Jean Bell. *Closed:* One week for New Year's. *Recreational facilities:* Riding at the hotel; golf, tennis, salmon and seatrout fishing, and hunting nearby. *Other facilities:* Lounge, sun lounge, cocktail bar, garden. *Rooms:* 10, 8 with bath, all with telephone and TV; 1 self-catering cottage; some rooms suitable for wheelchair guests. 3-day reduction; off-season rates November through March; discount for children under 14 sharing. Inexpensive to moderate. *Restaurant service:* Luncheon, snacks, tea, dinner. *Credit cards:* Amex, Diners, Master, Visa. *How to get there:* From the south on A74, take the third sign marked Lockerbie and find hotel signposted. From the north, take the first sign marked Lockerbie and cross over the highway. *Telephone:* (057 62) 2427.

Nairn, Highland

CLIFTON HOTEL

I am one of those who always think it fun to be in Scotland.

Hilaire Belloc, 1942

This romantic hotel of unusual character seems to be a country house but is within walking distance of everything in town. "Theatrical" is a word often used to describe its style. The rooms are warmed by vivacious colors, as well as by log fires. Hand-blocked wallpaper sets off fine Victorian antiques and chintz-and velvet-covered furniture; the walls are embellished with paintings and gilt-framed mirrors. Service and comfort get high marks. J. Gordon Macintyre is responsible for this long-established hotel's present exuberant charm. He enjoys telling stories of its Victorian past.

In the dining room, main courses include some unusual ones but also standard roasts for the less adventurous. Beds are made up with Continental quilts, but if you prefer sheets and blankets, as we do, ask for them when you reserve your room. The old custom of bringing an early-morning cup of tea to your bedroom is still followed here, and a full breakfast may be eaten in your bedroom or in the dining room, which faces the sea. If you are passing through Nairn, this is a good spot for lunch or afternoon tea.

No visitor to Scotland should miss nearby Culloden, now a peaceful tract of moorland, where the exhausted Jacobites under Bonnie Prince Charlie suffered a terrible slaughter at the hands of the red-coated army of the English Hanoverian king in 1746. An audio-visual presentation at the Visitor's Centre tells of the battle and the history of Scotland.

Proprietor: J. Gordon Macintyre. *Closed:* November through February. *Recreational facilities:* Ocean swimming at the hotel; indoor pool, tennis, and squash nearby. *Other facilities:* Drawing room, writing room, TV room, cocktail bar, garden. *Rooms:* 16 with bath. Moderate to expensive. *Restaurant service:* Snacks, tea, dinner (coat and tie required). *Credit cards:* Amex, Diners, Master, Visa. *How to get there:* Nairn is on Route A96 east of Inverness. Take Marine Road toward the ocean. Turn left on Seafield Street. The hotel will be on your left. Guests arriving by train in Nairn may telephone the hotel to be picked up. Guests can be met at the Inverness airport. *Telephone:* (0667) 53119.

ROSEDALE HOTEL

> From the lone shieling of the misty island
> Mountains divide us, and the waste of seas—
> Yet still the blood is strong, the heart is Highland
> And we in dreams behold the Hebrides.
> *John Galt*

The Rosedale Hotel is directly on the waterfront in the heart of Portree, the capital of Skye, largest island of the Inner Hebrides. It consists of several whitewashed, early-nineteenth-century buildings that were built against a sharp slope. Entrance is at the top level from the street side that faces the village center and at the bottom level from the quay along the harbor. Erratic stairways go up and down every which way. Furnishings are plain modern, but the atmosphere of the hotel, decorated with pretty colors, is light and airy, pleasant and friendly. The dining room faces the water on the middle level. Ask for a bedroom that has the same harbor view.

If you are using a BritRail pass, you may think you cannot reach Portree, but a bus that will take you there meets the ferry that crosses to Skye frequently from Kyle of Lochalsh on the mainland. The 30-mile drive from ferry to hotel brings into view brooding mountains that rise straight from the sea, but Portree itself is a lively little town visited by yachts and fishing boats of all kinds. When you return to the mainland, you will carry with you happy memories of your visit to the fabled Isle of the Mist.

Proprietor: Hugh Andrew. *Closed:* October through April. *Recreational facilities:* Indoor pool, tennis, and squash a short walk away. *Other facilities:* Lounge, TV lounge, cocktail bar. *Rooms:* 23 with bath, telephone, TV, and tea-making. Off-season rates. Inexpensive to moderate. *Restaurant service:* Snacks, tea, dinner. *How to get there:* Take the ferry to the Isle of Skye from either Mallaig or Kyle of Lochalsh. Take Route A850 north to Portree. Or take the train to Kyle of Lochalsh, ferry to Kyleakin, then bus to Portree. *Telephone:* (0478) 2531. [T]

St Andrews, Fife

RUFFLETS HOTEL

> In the fields called the Links, the citizens . . . divert
> themselves at a game called golf . . . they use a curious
> kind of bats tipped with horn, and small balls of
> leather, stuffed with feathers. . . . This they strike
> with such force . . . from one hole to another, that
> they will fly to an incredible distance.
>
> *Tobias Smollett,* 1771

The historic university city St Andrews is known to golfers all over the
world as the home of the Royal and Ancient Golf Club. Mary, Queen

of Scots, played golf, as did Charles I and James II. In 1834 William IV approved the title "Royal and Ancient" for the course at St Andrews. Visitors may play the game on its hallowed turf.

Rufflets Hotel, on the outskirts of the city, is delightful. To the once private mansion was added a large cocktail bar, where we enjoyed talking first to students from St Andrews University, then to a group of men from all over Britain who meet here once each year to golf together. Walls are decorated with a collection of prints by Sir William Russel Flint.

Vegetables from the hotel's garden are served at candlelit dinners in a dining room overlooking lawns with a nine-hole putting green. A small stream wanders across the back of the large garden, crossed by little bridges along the garden paths, and an extensive flower garden supplies bright bouquets daily.

You should apply for a starting time at the Old Course as early as possible. Each player must produce a valid handicap certificate and/or a letter of introduction from his home club. Write for information about advance reservations to the hotel. We were able to play without having made a reservation by giving our names to the hotel desk before 2 P.M. The hotel calls the starter, and at 3 P.M. names are drawn for cancellations for the next day's starting times. If you don't win one of these, ask the hotel to arrange for you to play on one of the other three courses: Jubilee, Eden, and New. They are open Sundays, but the Old Course is not.

For nongolfers there are sandy beaches and good shops. A visit to the St Andrew Woollen Mills, beside the Old Course, is a must.

Manager: Peter Aretz. *Closed:* January. *Recreational facilities:* 9-hole putting green at the hotel; ocean swimming, tennis, sauna, riding, golf, and freshwater fishing a short drive away. *Facilities for children:* Baby-listening. *Other facilities:* 2 lounges, cocktail bar, garden. *Rooms:* 21 with bath, TV, tea-making, and telephone. Suitable for wheelchair guests. 3-day reduction; 2-day breaks; free for children under 10 sharing; Christmas and New Year's programs. Moderate to expensive. *Restaurant service:* Luncheon, snacks, supper, dinner. *Credit cards:* Amex, Diners, Master, Visa. How to get there: The hotel is on Strathkinness Low Road, Route B939. *Telephone:* (0334) 72594.[T]

PHILIPBURN HOUSE HOTEL

A mist of memory broods and floats,
The Border waters flow;
The air is full of ballad notes,
Borne out of long ago.

Andrew Lang, 1899

Philipburn House is one of the friendliest hotels in Scotland, and a must for anyone traveling with children. Normally those without children do not seek out family hotels, but they shouldn't avoid this one. Supervised hiking and horseback riding, playgrounds, game rooms, and early suppers take care of young guests so well that the rest of us can enjoy both socializing in lounge or bar and gourmet dining without noisy interruption.

Jim Hill, architect turned innkeeper, skillfully modified and added to an eighteenth-century house set in 4 acres of garden. The inn is now an attractive and unusual mix of modern furnishings, antiques, wicker, and bamboo. Some new bedrooms with pine ceilings have sliding glass doors that lead to private terraces overlooking a swimming pool. There are several family suites with bunkrooms for the children.

Jim is also a dedicated chef and supervises cooking that is worth remembering. The menu might include casserole of game with oranges, grouse wrapped in bacon, Dover sole simmered in butter and vermouth, and salmon and trout from the nearby Ettrick and Yarrow rivers. For dessert, such delights as fresh peach cake laced with peach brandy, Westmorland nut-and-raisin flan, or Grand Marnier soufflé make choosing difficult. Wines are Anne's hobby; an extraordinary cellar offers nearly three hundred—some dating back to 1929.

A jovial personality about the hotel is David Fordyce, who leads guests on rambles into the hills, tends bar wearing his kilt, and recites native poetry in Scots dialect. He enjoys sharing with guests his extensive knowledge of the history and legends of the Border. Sir Walter Scott's home, Abbotsford, is just 4 miles away, and the great abbeys of Dryburgh, Jedburgh, and Melrose are all within a very short drive. Even nonshoppers will want to go to the nearby woolen mill that offers bargains in Scottish tweeds.

If you can't stay, stop for lunch or for afternoon tea, which is served by the pool or under garden trees when the weather is warm enough. This distinctive hotel is just over the border from England and the place for those who have time for only a dip into Scotland.

Proprietors: Jim and Anne Hill. *Recreational facilities:* Outdoor pool and badminton at the hotel; indoor pool a short walk away; tennis, riding, hunting, golf, shooting, and salmon and trout fishing a short drive away. *Facilities for children:* Baby-sitting and -listening; children's playground. *Other facilities:* Lounge, TV lounge, cocktail bar, games room, garden. *Rooms:* 16 with bath, TV, and tea-making. Suitable for wheelchair guests. 2-night reduction; 2-day breaks; reduction for children sharing; free under 10. Moderate. *Restaurant service:* Luncheon, snacks, tea, dinner. *Credit cards:* Amex, Diners, Visa. *How to get there:* Leave Selkirk going west on Route A706. The hotel is on the right. *Telephone:* (0750) 20747.

WALES

CONRAH COUNTRY HOTEL

In their manners the people could not be more amiable
than the English, who are as amiable as possible, but
they seemed brighter and gayer. This remained their
effect to the last in Aberystwyth.

William Dean Howells, 1909

Aberystwyth, home of the University of Wales and the National
Library, is a large summer resort with a long promonade along the
beach. There is much for older children and teen-agers to enjoy—games
such as crazy golf, indoor arcades, windsurfing instruction, pony-
trekking. There is a carnival atmosphere at large beachfront resorts in
July and August, and a visit to one is something typically British to
be experienced.

But rather than stay in the town, we prefer to find a nearby country-
house hotel. Conrah Country Hotel is the nicest in the area. Once a
country mansion, this friendly place has comfortable lounges, with log
fires on cool evenings and bay windows that afford views across valleys
to distant mountains. Spacious bedrooms in the main house are more
expensive but preferable to somewhat motel-like rooms in the annex.
The Headings take pride in their restaurant which attracts many area
patrons.

A popular excursion is to take one of "The Great Little Trains of
Wales" through the fine scenery of the Vale of Rheidol for 12 miles
to Devil's Bridge, where there are spectacular water falls.

Proprietors: John and Patricia Heading *Closed:* 3 days at Christmas.
Recreational facilities: Indoor pool, sauna and table tennis at the hotel;
ocean swimming, tennis, squash, riding, deep-sea fishing, wind-surfing,
boat hire and boat trips nearby. *Other facilities:* 2 lounges, cocktail bar,
garden. *Rooms:* 20 doubles, 2 singles, with bath, 2 doubles sharing
bath, all with TV, telephone, tea-making; elevator; 3-night reduction;
2-night breaks October to mid-June; no children under 8. Moderate
to expensive. *Restaurant service:* Luncheon, snacks, tea, dinner (coat
and tie Saturday evening). *Credit cards:* Amex, Diners, Master, Visa.
How to get there: The hotel is 3 miles south of Aberystwyth on Route
A487. It will meet the train at Aberystwyth. *Telephone:* (0970) 617941

[T]

Bontddu, Gwynedd

BONTDDU HALL

> You look inland where the salt tide swirls and eddies,
> towards the mountains round Dolgelley. They lie fold-
> ed against one another in long gentle line, flaming with
> gorse, green with grass, the darker belts of woodland
> climbing in the hollows.
>
> *H. V. Morton*

This jewel of a hotel, surely one of the finest in Wales, is a fresh, blithe place, an endearing mixture of elegance and informality. It began life as an imposing Victorian baronial pile set on a height. Its decor, encompassing a surprising range of styles, is exceptional. Some rooms are grand, with heavy, carved antiques. A lounge, in great contrast, has white bamboo furniture covered with pastel pinks, greens, and yellows, surprising and effective under a wood-beamed ceiling. A window wall of the dining room, which has won high recommendations, gives views over the Mawddach estuary and Cader Idris range of mountains, the scene described by H. V. Morton above. Several acres of cultivated gardens are enhanced by stone walls and statuary.

Many hotels boast that each bedroom is different, but here the variations are enormous. Some have draped beds and lush colors; one has brass beds and summery green and white matching wallpaper and curtains; each stylish modern lodge room in a new addition on an elevated site has a magnificent view from a private sun balcony. When we think of Bontddu Hall (pronounced Bonthee), we see the lovely rooms, the magnificent trees, the dramatic views, and we wish we were there.

Proprietors: Magaretta and Michael Ball. *Closed:* January to late March. *Recreational facilities:* Ocean swimming, riding, boat rental (canoe, row, sail, motor), boat trips, and deep-sea fishing a short drive away. *Other facilities:* Drawing room, lounge, sun parlor, cocktail bar, public bar, garden. *Rooms:* 24 with bath, TV, and telephone. Ground-floor rooms. Off-season rates (almost 50% less); 3-day reduction; breaks. No children under 3; children under 16 free if sharing. Moderate. *Restaurant service:* Luncheon, snacks, tea, dinner. *Credit cards:* Amex, Diners, Master, Visa. *How to get there:* The hotel is on Route A496 between Barmouth and Dolgellau. *Telephone:* (034 149) 661.[T]

GLIFFAES COUNTRY HOUSE

I care not, I, to fish in seas
Fresh river best my mind do please.

William Basse, 1653

On the terrace we basked in the spring sun. Lawns rolled rather steeply away to where the River Usk gleamed silver far below, an angler on its banks casting for salmon. Across the river, cattle grazed placidly on verdant meadows. This is a place to relax, surrounded by nature's beauty. Fishing is a main attraction. The hotel owns more than 2 miles of the Usk, reputed to be one of the best salmon and trout rivers in the British Isles.

A long driveway flanked by showy rhododendrons leads to the imposing house, built as a private mansion in 1885. One of its two distinctive towers holds a chiming clock, silent during the night. Twenty-seven acres of parkland and gardens contain some of the rarest and most beautiful trees in Wales. Despite its outward magnificence, the Gliffaes is not a luxury hotel, but it is comfortable and pleasant. Mr. and Mrs. Brabner, resident owners, encourage friendliness.

Afternoon tea is set out buffet style; the country-style food served here is very good. Our bedroom was large, with a balcony that had the same lovely view we enjoyed from the terrace.

This hotel is set in a national park in gentle mountains called the Brecon Beacons, unspoiled countryside ideal for the bird-watcher. Pony-trekking through its hills and valleys can be arranged. On Llangorse Lake, 8 miles away, sailing and water-skiing are available.

Proprietors: Mr. and Mrs. Nick Brabner. *Closed:* January 1–March 15. *Recreational facilities:* Tennis with a pro available, river swimming, salmon and trout fishing, and nine-hole putting green at the hotel; riding, indoor pool, boating, and water-skiing nearby. *Other facilities:* Drawing room, lounge, TV room, cocktail bar, billiard room, sun room, garden. *Rooms:* 19 with bath, telephone, and tea-making. Reduction; 2-day breaks. Inexpensive to moderate. *Restaurant service:* Luncheon, snacks, tea, dinner. *Credit cards:* Amex, Master, Visa. *How to get there:* Take Route A40 west from Abergavenny to about 2 1/2 miles beyond Crickhowell. Turn left and follow signs to Gliffaes House, 1 mile farther on. *Telephone:* (0874) 730371.

Crugybar, Dyfed

GLANRANNELL PARK HOTEL

These are the things I prize
And hold of dearest worth;
Light of the sapphire skies,
Peace of the silent hills,
Shelter of forests, comforts of the grass,
Music of birds, murmur of little rills,
And after showers,
The smell of flowers,
And of the good brown earth,
And best of all, along the way,
Friendship and mirth.

Henry Van Dyke, 1892

The things prized by Henry Van Dyke, in his little poem above, he would find at this peaceful, friendly hotel today. Bronwen and David Davies owned a small London hotel before they returned to Wales some years ago to open this country house. Would that all hotels could boast such agreeable and obliging proprietors.

The house is surrounded by lawns and overlooks a lake. Books are distributed among the pleasant, comfy rooms that are plainly decorated, with linen antimacassars protecting floral upholstery. Good country cooking that includes homemade bread uses local produce whenever possible. Afternoon tea is a specialty, with Welsh cakes and scones. Picnic lunches are provided when desired. The wine cellar boasts a good selection.

David raises Welsh cobs on his 23 acres. Glanrannell Park bears a plaque for being the house that raised the prize pony Dyoll Starlight in about 1900, the Welsh stud from which most registered Welsh ponies are descended. A flock of Black Welsh mountain sheep share the paddocks. David, who speaks fluent Welsh, makes Welsh musical instruments.

Proprietors: Bronwen and David Davies. *Recreational facilities:* Salmon and sea-trout fishing and riding nearby. *Facilities for children:* Baby-sitting. *Other facilities:* Sitting room, TV room, cocktail bar, garden. *Rooms:* 8, 5 with bath and tea-making. Reduction for children sharing (free under 2). Inexpensive. *Restaurant service:* Snacks, tea, dinner. *How to get there:* The hotel is on Route 4302 just south of Route 482, between Llanwrda and Lampeter. *Telephone:* (05583) 230.

YNYSHIR HALL

The kiss of the sun for pardon,
The song of the bird for mirth,
One is nearer God's heart in a garden
Than anywhere else on earth.

Anonymous

Surrounded by the Ynyshir Bird Reserve, Ynyshir Hall is a sixteenth-century manor house surrounded by 10 acres of gardens, profuse with rhododendron, camellia, and heather. It's truly a peaceful spot.

Inside the pale pink building, rooms are spacious and comfortable, with some antique furnishings. Log fires add to the atmosphere of warmth and welcome, and bedrooms are named for flowers. Dinner includes vegetables and fruit from a walled kitchen garden. If you can't stay, you might stop in for morning coffee or afternoon tea with homemade cookies.

Whether you want to fish in the adjacent River Dovey, bird watch in the Ynyshir Bird Reserve, rent clubs and play golf, or sit in a bay window admiring the view, the beauty of Wales will stay with you long after you leave.

Proprietors: Jane and Richard Allison. *Recreational facilities:* River swimming at the hotel; golf, boat hire, boat trips on the River Dovey, riding, and ocean swimming nearby. *Facilities for children:* Baby-listening. *Other facilities:* Lounge, cocktail bar, garden. *Rooms:* 12 with bath; some suitable for wheelchair guests; Christmas program; Moderate. *Restaurant service:* Luncheon, tea, dinner. *Credit cards:* Amex, Diners, Master, Visa. *How to get there:* The hotel is signposted on Route A487 between Machynlleth and Aberystwyth. Guests can be met at Machynlleth train station at no charge. *Telephone:* (065 474) 209.

Glyn Ceiriog, Clwyd

GOLDEN PHEASANT

> Oh, the wild hills of Wales, the land of old renown
> and of wonder.
>
> *George Borrow*

This unusual country inn is renowned for the excellence of the sports it offers. Imagine yourself riding through heather, purple against a blue sky. Experienced riders go off in small groups, beginners are given lessons by expert instructors. The Turners raise registered Welsh cobs.

Shooting? All kinds are catered to, from covert shooting to grouse driving, and for partridge, pheasant, or mallards in season. Fishing? Catch salmon on a privately owned beat of the Welsh Dee and on the Severn; sea trout and brown trout on the Ceiriog; rainbow and brown trout on Lake Vyrnwy, an hour away through magnificent country. Anyone serious about these sports should write well in advance, get the brochures, and make arrangements.

Part of this congenial inn dates back to 1755, when it was a brewery. Jennifer Turner Gibourg is acclaimed for her cooking, which features Welsh lamb, fresh trout, and game in season, "roasted, casseroled, and in crusty pies." Guests come for the homemade soups and Dee salmon. Desserts are home-baked, from apple pie to luscious cakes. Under the 1775 beams in the bar, a fire in a grate sets off burnished horse brasses, and walls are hung with fox heads, guns, and sporting prints.

Each season brings its own delights: in spring, apple trees blossom, Welsh lambs and Welsh foals frolic; in summer, daylight lasts until after ten, for sitting in the garden; in autumn, crisp days sparkle and leaves turn to many hues; in winter, the hunt meets and hearty winter teas are enjoyed by the fire.

Proprietors: The Turner family. *Recreational facilities:* Riding, hunting, fishing, shooting, and guided walks from the hotel. *Facilities for children:* Riding lessons. *Other facilities:* Lounge, cocktail bar, public bar, garden. *Rooms:* 19 with bath, TV, telephone, and tea-making. 2-day reduction; breaks; children under 18 free if sharing. Christmas program; New Year's program. Moderate. *Restaurant service:* Luncheon, snacks, dinner. *Credit cards:* Amex, Diners, Master. *How to get there:* Take Route A5 to Chirk, then Route B4500 to Glyn Ceiriog. Guests can be met at the Chirk railway station. *Telephone:* (069 172) 281. *Agent in the United States:* Josephine Barr.   [T]

THE WEST ARMS

> Everything the landscape painter could want was to
> be found in North Wales.
>
> *Richard Wilson,* 1775

In this land of song and rugged hills, there is a remote valley, little known to Americans, where you will find an inn of the picture-book kind. Much of its charm derives from simple country things—the River Ceiriog tumbling through the village, the rolling, heather-covered hills, the gamboling of new lambs in the spring, the bleating of sheep the only sound to enliven the solitude.

The inn specializes in serving such good Welsh food as spring lamb, fresh salmon, pheasant and other game in season, and home-cooked desserts, with a choice of wines from an extensive list. Pretty posies ornament the tables. Handhewn beams give character to the rooms, where brass and polished mahogany reflect the flames from the cavernous fireplaces. The pub, furnished with oak, including a carved confessional, has been honored as a Pub of the Year for Wales.

You will be equally well taken care of at the only other hotel in the village, as both are now owned by the Alexanders. It is the sixteenth-century Hand Hotel, as charming as is the West Arms.

Proprietors: Carolyn and Tim Alexander. *Recreational facilities:* Tennis and fishing at the hotel; golf and riding nearby. *Other facilities:* Lounge, TV lounge, cocktail bar, public bar, garden. *Rooms:* 14, 8 with bath. Suitable for wheelchair guests. 2-night reduction. Christmas and New Year's program. Inexpensive to moderate. *Restaurant service:* Luncheon, snacks, tea, dinner. *Credit card:* Amex, Diners, Master, Visa. *How to get there:* Take Route A5 to Chirk, turn at the church onto Route B4500 for Glyn Ceiriog, and continue about 11 miles to Llanarmon D.C. *Telephone:* (069 176) 665.

Penmaenpool, Gwynedd

GEORGE III HOTEL

> Then come who pine for peace and pleasure,
> Away from counter, court and school,
> Spend here your measure of time and treasure,
> And taste the treats of Penmaenpool.
> *Gerard Manley Hopkins*

Right on the water there's a charming little inn that was once a ship chandlery. Sailing ships from here brought slate to the United States and returned with hardwoods to build more ships. Stone benches beside the estuary make a great place to eat lunch while you watch rowboats bobbing at moorings. In the bar you'll find a large selection of snacks—homemade steak and kidney pie, toasted sandwiches, pizzas, and an assortment of salads from a buffet. The dining room, known for good food, specializes in local duck, pheasant, lobster, sea trout, and salmon.

The poet Gerard Manley Hopkins is said to have written the verse above in the guest book when he stayed at the hotel. Its brochure reads, "Our aim is to provide an informal atmosphere coupled with good food and wine, so that you may rejoin the hurly burly of life refreshed." This wonderfully cozy inn succeeds admirably. A cavernous fireplace with an enormous inglenook gives great character to an Old World lounge. The bars hold a wealth of brass and old blue and white china. Traditional bedrooms in delightful strong colors are well furnished. Those in a Victorian building next to the inn are larger, with excellent modern baths.

Proprietor: Gail Hall. *Closed:* Christmas. *Recreational facilities:* Ocean swimming, riding, boat trips, and deep-sea fishing a short drive away. *Facilities for children:* Baby-listening. *Other facilities:* Lounge, cocktail bar, public bar. *Rooms:* 12, 7 with bath, all with TV and tea-making. 3-day reduction; 2-day breaks; discount for children under 11 sharing. Inexpensive to moderate. *Restaurant service:* Early and late snacks, dinner. *Credit cards:* Amex, Carte Blanche, Diners, Master, Visa. *How to get there:* Penmaenpool is west of Dolgellau on Route A493, at the bridge that crosses the Mawddach estuary. *Telephone:* (0341) 422 525. [T]

Penmorfa, Gwynedd

BWLCH-Y-FEDWEN

There was no such place, and there never had been any such place, as the hostelry of the coaching age for creature comforts and good service.

Charles Harper, 1906

The friendly Bridges will make you feel welcome right away in this snug guest house, once a coaching inn dating back to 1664. The lounge is really a parlor with Victorian and Edwardian furniture and much bric-a-brac on tables, some with tops of needlepoint under glass. Bookcases with interesting books about Wales line one wall, and others display pictures in heavy Victorian frames, Coalport plates, and Royal Crown Derby ornaments. It's a congenial setting where guests talk to each other around a coal fire in the grate. Two golden retrievers not allowed into the parlor were so polite they stood and talked to us from a doorway, tails slowly waving.

The old coaching inn atmosphere is strong in the candlelit dining room, which has stone walls, low beams, and a large hearth. We were very happy with the duckling with stuffing and applesauce, but there was also roast beef with Yorkshire pudding and horseradish sauce. Don't skip dessert—brandy gateau, cherry cream shortcake, hazel meringue.

Plan to visit Caernarvon Castle not far away. We do not tour every castle; we would rather stay in those converted to hotels than take guided tours, but at Caernarvon Castle a guided tour isn't required. We wandered through the vast stone ruin, trying to imagine life here in the Middle Ages. We twisted up tight, spiral stone stairs that sometimes ended abruptly, picked our way through dim passages to turn a corner and find no roof, peered out through slits through which long-bowmen once showered arrows to repulse the enemy, saw the room where the present Prince Charles was invested as Prince of Wales, and heard the melodious voices of chattering groups of Welsh schoolchildren. It's a fascinating memory.

Proprietors: Gwyneth and Arthur Bridge. *Closed:* November through March. *Recreational facilities:* Ocean swimming a short drive away. *Other facilities:* Drawing room, TV lounge, sun parlor, cocktail bar, garden. *Rooms:* 6 with bath. 3-day reduction. No children under 12. Inexpensive. *How to get there:* The lodging is on Route A487, the Porthmadog-Caernarvon road. *Telephone:* (0766) 512975.

Talsarnau, Gwynedd

MAES-Y-NEUADD HOTEL

> A morsel of genuine history is a thing so rare as to be always valuable.
>
> *Thomas Jefferson*

Maes-y-Neuadd has been designated by the government as a building of both architectural and historic interest. People first lived within some of its walls in the fourteenth century. Three centuries later it was Oliver Cromwell's headquarters during a Welsh campaign, and the name of the Cromwell Bar commemorates those times.

Some rooms are furnished with antiques, greetings are warm, and the atmosphere is peaceful. Cooking is good, with vegetables picked from the hotel's own gardens. We enjoyed a delicious afternoon tea on a terrace in the sun. From the hilltop setting, we gazed across fields and over treetops to sparkling Cardigan Bay, admiring the same glorious views that had been familiar to Cromwell and his Roundheads.

Mount Snowdon, highest mountain in England or Wales, where the first successful Mount Everest team trained, is only 13 miles away. You won't need to climb to get to its top. The only mountain rack railway in the British Isles will take you to the summit to see some of the grandest scenery in Britain. On clear days, the Wicklow hills in Ireland and the Isle of Man are visible.

Proprietors: June and Michael Slatter and Olive and Malcolm Horsfall. *Closed:* January. *Recreational facilities:* Golf, tennis, riding, and swimming in ocean, lake, river, or indoor pool a short drive away. *Other facilities:* Lounge, cocktail bar, garden. *Rooms:* 15 with bath and TV; 1 suite. 2-night reduction. Breaks. No children under 7. Moderate to expensive. *Restaurant service:* Luncheon, tea, dinner. *Credit cards:* Master, Visa. *How to get there:* Maes-y-Neuadd (pronounced Mice-er-Nayath) is signposted on Route B4573 between Harlech and Portmadoc and is about half a mile off the road. *Telephone:* (0766) 780 200. *Agent in the United States:* BTH.   [T]

INDEX OF INNS
(WITH POSTAL CODES & RATES)

Postal codes have been listed following the name of the inn. The prices listed in this index were those for two people in high season in 1988. Unless otherwise indicated, they included breakfast (usually a full breakfast but occasionally a Continental breakfast). Rates are given in pounds, with their dollar equivalents in parentheses. The dollar exchange rate was figured at $1.69 to the pound. Where two prices are given, they are for the lowest- and highest-priced double rooms. Many establishments offer lower prices off season. Always ask for the current rates before you make reservations.

The following abbreviations are used:

    EP = European Plan — no breakfast
    MAP = Modified American Plan — rates included dinner and breakfast

Angel Hotel (1P33 1LT), 53; rates: 70-85 (119-144) EP
Appletree Holme Farm (LA12 8EL), 34; rates: 82-88 (139-149) MAP
Arundell Arms (PL16 0AA), 117; rates: 50-62 (85-105)
Aynsome Manor (LA11 6HH), 56; rates: 73-78 (123-132) MAP
Bailiffscourt Hotel (BN17 5RW), 65; rates: 95-135 (161-228)
Banchory Lodge (AB3 3H6), 195; rates: from 73 (from 124)
Bay Tree (OX8 4LW), 51; rates: 54-70 (91-119)
Beechfield House (SN12 7PU), 29; rates: 80-90 (136-152)
Bell Inn (HP22 5HP), 27; rates: 83-104 (141-176)
Bibury Court (GL7 5NT), 30; rates: 51-58 (86-97)
Black Horse Inn (PE10 0LY), 97; rates: 55 (93)
Bontddu Hall (LL40 2SU), 231; rates: 56-65 (95-110)
Bootham Bar Hotel (YO1 2EH), 185; rates: 48 (81)
Boscundle Manor (PL25 3RL), 151; rates: 66-77 (112-130)
Broadway Hotel (WR12 7AA), 46; rates: 56-72 (95-122)
Browns' Hotel, (EH41 3RD), 213; rates: 51-56 (86-95)
Bull Hotel (CO10 9JG), 128; rates: 65 (110) EP
Burghope Manor (BA15 2LB), 183; rates: 50-60 (85-101)
Bwlch-y-Fedwen (LL49 9RY), 243; rates: 55-60 (93-101) MAP
Clifton Hotel (IV12 4HW), 222; rates: 68-76 (115-129)
Close, (GL8 8AQ), 163; rates: 83-135 (140-228)
Collin House (WR12 7PB), 47; rates: 58-65 (97-110)
Combe House (EX14 0AD), 89; rates: 66-85 (112-144)
Connaught, The (WIY 6AL), 121; rates on request
Conrah Country Hotel (SY23 4DF), 230; rates: 57-77 (97-130)
Court, The, (DT2 9NH), 87; rates: 47 (80) MAP
Crosby Lodge (CA6 4QZ), 75; rates: 69-77 (115-130)
Crown Hotel (BA5 2RP), 172; rates: 49-58 (82-97)
Culloden House (IV1 2NZ), 214; rates: 110-149 (186-251)
Dedham Vale Hotel (CO7 6HW), 77; rates: 75-85 (127-144)
Dryfesdale Hotel (DG11 2SF), 221 rates: 38-48 (64-81)
Dunain Park (IV3 6JN), 215; rates: 75-88 (127-149)

Send us your name and address...
...and we'll send you a free gift.

If you purchased this book, we'd like your name and address for our mailing list. Just supply the information below, and we'll send you your free gift.

I purchased this book at:

- ☐ Atticus
- ☐ Barnes & Noble
- ☐ B. Dalton Booksellers
- ☐ Bookland
- ☐ Books Inc.
- ☐ Crown Books
- ☐ Encore Books
- ☐ Hunter's Books
- ☐ J.K. Gill

- ☐ Kroch's & Brentano's
- ☐ Lauriats
- ☐ Marshall Field & Co.
- ☐ Paperback Booksmith
- ☐ Readmore
- ☐ Stacy's
- ☐ Taylors
- ☐ Upstart Crow & Co.
- ☐ Waldenbooks

Other:_____   (City)_____

I purchased this book on (approximate date):_____

Please send my free gift to:

Name:_____

Street or Box:_____

City_____ State_____ Zip_____

Please mail to:
The Compleat Traveler, c/o Burt Franklin & Co., Inc.
235 East 44th St., New York, N.Y. 10017 U.S.A.

Limit: One per customer.   **Limited time offer.**

THE COMPLEAT TRAVELER'S READER REPORT

To: *The Compleat Traveler*
  c/o Burt Franklin & Co., Inc.
  P.O. Box 856
  New York, New York 10014, U.S.A.

Dear Compleat Traveler:

I have used your book in _____ (country or region).
I would like to offer the following ☐ new recommendation, ☐ comment,
☐ suggestion, ☐ criticism, ☐ or complaint about:

Name of Country Inn or Hotel:

_____

Address: _____

_____

Comments:

Day of my visit: _____   Length of stay: _____

From (name): _____

Address _____

_____ Telephone: _____